"No matter how you feel about your mother-in-law, *The Daughter-In-Law's Survival Guide* will help you better understand and approach one of the most significant—and unexplored—relationships in your life."

—Lisa Pollak, Pulitzer-prize winning
features writer, *Baltimore Sun*

"Every page of *The Daughter-in-Law's Survival Guide* offers dazzling stories we can learn from."

—Jo Giese, author of *A Woman's Path*,
and award-winning host of *Breaking
the Mold,* heard on Marketplace, Public
Radio International

"*The Daughter-In-Law's Survival Guide* reaches into the dark spaces of family life to illuminate both the fears and promises of in-law relationships. It challenges long-held notions about the solidarity of women, exposing the vulnerability of even the most well-intended extended family relations. The book's insights are invaluable to a broader interpretation of marriage and family function and dysfunction."

—Katrina Bell McDonald, Ph.D., Associate
Professor, Dept. of Sociology, The
Johns Hopkins University

When women are trying to cope with a problem, struggling through a major life transition, or just in need of a reality check and a little healing support, we go straight to our friends. Each of the books in the *Women Talk About* series reflects the experiences of dozens of women from diverse backgrounds, whose words are accompanied by provocative insights from the latest research. Often funny, sometimes painful, and always honest, their powerful voices reassure us that we're not alone; offer guidance and wisdom; and show us how to connect back to the woman we want to be.

The *Daughter-in-Law's*
SURVIVAL GUIDE

EVERYTHING YOU NEED

TO KNOW ABOUT RELATING

TO YOUR MOTHER-IN-LAW

EDEN UNGER BOWDITCH
& AVIVA SAMET, PSY.D.

New Harbinger Publications, Inc.

Publisher's Note

This publication is designed to provide accurate and authoritative information in regard to the subject matter covered. It is sold with the understanding that the publisher is not engaged in rendering psychological, financial, legal, or other professional services. If expert assistance or counseling is needed, the services of a competent professional should be sought.

Distributed in the U.S.A. by Publishers Group West; in Canada by Raincoast Books; in Great Britain by Airlift Book Company, Ltd.; in South Africa by Real Books, Ltd.; in Australia by Boobook; and in New Zealand by Tandem Press.

Copyright © 2002 by Eden Unger Bowditch & Aviva Samet
New Harbinger Publications, Inc.
5674 Shattuck Avenue
Oakland, CA 94609

Cover design by Amy Shoup
Cover image by Dan Chavkin/Stone
Edited by Kayla Sussell
Text design by Michele Waters

ISBN 1-57224-281-7 Paperback

Printed in the United States of America

New Harbinger Publications' Web site address:
www.newharbinger.com

04   03   02

10   9   8   7   6   5   4   3   2   1

First printing

This book is dedicated to our wonderful husbands, Nate Unger Bowditch and James Eliot Matanky, whom we love and adore. And without whom we would not, in fact, be daughters-in-law.

Contents

Part I: The Good

When she was good she was very, very good ...

Chapter 1

Part II: The Bad

But when she was bad ...

Part III: The Ugly
She was horrid!

Acknowledgments

We would like to thank all of the daughters-in-law who shared their stories, both joyous and troubling, intimately and candidly. They were brave and opened up to us, going where many feared to go. But they did. Also, we would like to thank the experts in various fields who helped ensure the accuracy of our information, especially Dr. Teri Apter, George Davis, Dr. Layla Kassem; the dedicated people at New Harbinger for their wise decision making and thoughtful input, especially Lorna Garano, Heather G. Mitchener, Amy Shoup, Kayla Sussell, and Catharine Sutker. We would also like to thank those friends and acquaintances who were helpful and enthusiastic, encouraging us to proceed, including: Sandra Andreoli, Kristin Beck, and Judith Newman.

To our families (old and new) who were attentive and caring as we explored the lives of so many women and reflected on our own intimate relationships. To James, Nate, Julius, and Lyric for their infinite love and patience. For all of those who have expressed enthusiasm and anticipation for this book and to all of you who have found it.

Introduction

A Rose by Any Other Name ...

Belle-mère is French for mother-in-law. It is much more tactful than the bureaucratic sounding "in-law" that English attaches to our comparable term. *Belle-mère* has a pleasant ring, a warm feel to it. In French, it also means "stepmother" and the two terms are intrinsically linked. But when a widowed or divorced father remarries, his children are subject to the same odd placement that categorizes a "child-in-law." Should these children expect unconditional love from their new stepmother? Does the newly married pair expect to have a family that functions well just because they love one another? This is the predicament that both in-law and stepfamilies face.

Historically, the most maligned character in children's stories has always been the stepmother. They are relegated to the ranks of the ogre and evil witch. Mother-in-law jokes are as old as the institution and they are translatable and understood in every language on the planet. It makes you wonder, doesn't it?

As children we were randomly assigned to classrooms and forced to associate with a lot of disparate personalities. There were kids we hated and kids we loved and kids we could never remember. And for all the romantic memories we may cherish about our childhoods, most of us would run from the opportunity to relive those early days. Why?

Because it was hell having to spend every day for years and years forced to stand in line next to the stinky guy with the runny nose and peanut butter fingers just because his last name started with the same letter as yours.

When we got into middle school and then high school, it was easier to move away from such forced intimacies. However, we were still required to associate with people completely alien to us. By the time we reached college, or entered the working world, we were at least among others who were there by choice or opportunity.

Then came our serious relationships, lifelong commitments, and the relatives of our life partners. (You don't have to be "married" to have a "belle-mère." Life partners are life partners, common law or not. So face it, anyone in a committed relationship has to interact with in-laws as much as those with marriage licenses. When a woman displaces a man's mother as the number one woman in his life, by necessity, she must engage in the mother/daughter-in-law dynamic. If a woman's partner's mother is alive, that woman has a belle-mère.) According to a paper by Ramona Marotz-Baden and Deane Cowan (1987), "The intimate bond that mothers-in-law and daughters-in-law share with the son/husband (child/spouse) is often the only tie between them." We daughters in law may find ourselves holding hands with not one, but a whole family of strangers when all we really want is to hold hands with one special person. How is this supposed to work?

Not every in-law relationship is fraught with trials and tribulations. However, throughout history, the mother-in-law/ daughter-in-law relationship always has been a very challenging relationship. In fact, same-sex in-law relationships (i.e., fathers-in-law and sons-in-law/mothers-in-law and daughters-in-law) seem to have the greatest number of issues.

Overwhelmingly, the most difficult relationship seems to be between mothers-in-law and daughters-in-law. In many cultures, women are viewed as the "kinkeepers," the carriers and transmitters of family traditions and culture. They are expected to "really run the show" in the family. Mothers are traditionally the ones who weave together the separate strands that make up the fabric of family life, and who dictate what the environment of the home is to be. When it is time to pass this job on to the next generation, there can be dissension or apprehension among family members.

A successful relationship between mother-in-law and daughter-in-law is viewed in different ways in different cultures. In Paul Stirling's 1965 paper on household and family structure in a Turkish village, he found that the daughter-in-law "is expected to do all the more menial tasks in the household, and to wait on her mother-in-law." She is also supposed to be treated as a daughter.

To create some measure of balance, maintain order, or prevent familial disruption, Muslim law requires a mother-in-law not to feel jealousy, but a Muslim daughter-in-law is taught never to expect her husband to abandon his connection with his mother. According to Islam, a husband "cannot be made to forget his mother by his beautiful wife" thus taking her position of strength away. Dr. Layla Kassem said, "In Islam, the mother is the most esteemed in the human hierarchy." (2001). There is a saying from the Qu'ran that translates as "heaven is at the feet of all mothers" and it is the daughter-in-law's duty to make sure that this relationship is most observantly honored.

In many Asian cultures, informality is seen as disrespect, not as a sign of closeness. In China, a bride is expected to be subservient to her mother-in-law. Different cultures, as well as individual families, use language to imply tacit beliefs and expectations about intimacy between married families.

In Yiddish *machetunim* comes from the Hebrew word *mechutan,* meaning "relative (male or female) by marriage." The message is inclusive and refers to all members of both parties' immediate families; whereas in English, the parents of the couple are not considered "in-laws" of each other. Several cultures throughout the world practice avoidance of in-laws. For example, the Miskito of Central America require a mother-in-law to stay in her own section of the house when her son-in-law is present. In Kenya, Gusii brides do not receive much respect from their in-laws until they have given birth to a child.

It can be very helpful to read about how other people go through the same dance, albeit with different rhythms and different partners. Most of us have had experiences we wish we could have recorded, either to prove a point or to avoid making the same mistake again. We think that if only we had forevision instead of hindsight, we would be able to avoid catastrophe. If mothers-in-law and daughters-in law would just take the trouble to consider how even some of the most unconscious, nonmalicious actions can create problems, how seemingly innocent words or deeds can be terribly misunderstood, or how one act of viciousness can forever shatter relationships, perhaps they could avoid doing such damage to their own relationships.

To that end, we have gathered together interviews and stories from women who are daughters-in-law. These stories won't teach you how to be a perfect daughter-in-law or a perfect mother-in-law, for that matter. Neither will they prove that you can never be one. They offer a glimpse of what is possible. They offer you a chance to examine the pitfalls that can create a potentially agonizing human relationship.

Of course, not all mother-in-law relationships are negative. There are stellar and adoring relationships that are worthy of your attention. You may even find yourself in these pages, and different women's experiences may echo your own. You may see how an archetypal scene plays out with different actors and perhaps learn how such scenes can be rewritten or avoided altogether. Yes, we're all different, but we so often find ourselves acting out the very roles we think we could never, ever portray.

How We Came to Write This Book

As a writer (Eden) and a psychologist (Aviva), we approached this book from different disciplines. But the notion of collaborating on a project has always appealed to us, perhaps because we have known each other since the age of four and have been best friends ever since.

Shortly before Aviva's wedding, we began talking about what it means to be a daughter-in-law. Eden already had ten years' experience of being one. Our mothers had both had disappointing relationships with their mothers-in-law, so we had grown up regarding the prospect with some trepidation. We had many conversations on this topic. There was much we had to share, and it seemed that every woman we spoke to had something else to add to the discussion.

Ironically, given the ubiquitous presence of mother-in-law tales in society, there was not much in the literature on the mother-in-law/daughter-in-law relationship. Conspicuously absent was literature that offered the daughter-in-law's perspective. Given that each year about two and a half million marriages take place in the United States (Statistical Abstractions of the United States 2000), not counting the millions of nonlegally registered life partners, we know huge numbers of people are trying to figure out this relationship.

It is not our intention to tell women how to be better daughters-in-law. It was our intention to find out what goes on in the hearts of daughters-in-law and to convey that information to you. We wanted to see what makes someone judge a relationship as working well or failing. We wanted to see what we, and you, might glean from their insights.

The women you will meet in the following pages are a collection of fifty-three participating daughters-in-law who were interviewed in person and taped; were given written questionnaires and/or participated in a focus group. Most interviews took between one to three hours.

How to Use This Book

The book is divided into three sections called "The Good," "The Bad," and "The Ugly." Of course, we understand that matters usually are not so absolute when it comes to relationships. Generally, the groupings are established by how the daughter-in-law perceives her relationship with her mother-in-law.

If a woman believes that her relationship is "good," we honor that view and discuss it in a chapter in that section. However, we also may examine what she says, and we may think that her relationship is intrinsically problematic. We may believe that there are unaddressed conflicts in the relationship, which cause us to judge it anything but "good."

Although it is most important to understand how the daughter-in-law feels and what causes her to feel that way, some relationships simply need to be discussed in more than one section. We feel the reader will understand, for example, why a relationship that seems so "bad" might still appear in the "good" section, but the reader will also revisit those relationships and their various themes in more apt sections.

At the end of the chapters, you will find questions that have been selected to encourage reflection and exploration of your own relationship with your mother-in-law. Ultimately, we hope this book will facilitate an enriched and broadened view of the potential for this negatively stereotyped relationship. If that potential is transformed into opportunity by any of our readers, this project will have been a success.

Part I: The Good

When she was good she was very, very good ...

Chapter 1

Where Do We Stand?
An Overview

I was very relieved that my in-laws approved of us living together before marriage. I always considered myself lucky that they were so "cool."

—Joy

Her attitude is that she raised her children and now it's up to them to live their own lives while she goes about enjoying hers. I do believe she puts herself first . . . and, as far as I'm concerned, that's as it should be.

—Luzi

If the relationship in your life works and it feels right, then it can be called good. But you must be honest with yourself. "Good" does not mean the same to everyone. What may feel right from the inside may look strange from the outside. You must learn to recognize when particular issues need to be addressed. Even the best relationships cannot flourish without some attention being paid to them.

What Is a Good Relationship?

Good is a very vague term and obviously implies different things to different people. Whatever the particulars of the term may mean, they are positive. In a good relationship, both people feel positive levels of comfort and acceptance that allow them to function well. When it comes to mothers-in-law, the measure of what makes the relationship a good one varies greatly. The level of formality, intimacy, interaction, or participation considered comfortable depends on both women finding that level desirable. If either woman feels great discomfort with the other, the relationship cannot be considered a successful one.

For one woman, the sign of a good relationship with her mother-in law may be that her mother-in-law is intimately involved in her daily activities. To another woman, this kind of involvement may seem overbearing or invasive. Some daughters-in-law feel that good relationships with their mothers-in-law mean that the mothers-in-law do not impose themselves in any way in their sons' families. Still other women may experience the absence of their mother-in-law's involvement in their families' lives as neglect or rejection.

A good place to begin to create a good relationship is to be sensitive to each other's position. For example, Lea, who is an accountant, does not feel intimidated by or resentful of the time her husband spends with his mother. In fact, she encourages it. "Once a year my mother-in-law and her husband go on vacation for a week at the beach with all of their children. I don't go because my kids are in school then, but I encourage my husband to go because they all have a good time, and it is a time for her to enjoy her children all to herself. We go on other vacations with spouses and children and grandparents, but this is a good special time for them, and I think that's great."

Lea's mother-in-law was a good support when Lea needed someone to be there for her. "When I had each of the three children, she was there to help. She got the meals for everyone without being bothersome. She's overly generous at birthdays and Christmas with gifts she knows I'd like. But especially when something is bothering me, and I need to talk, she listens without comment and is very compassionate, not just with me but others as well."

Lea knows that things aren't always perfect and that, although she is "like a daughter," she is, in fact, not a daughter. When speaking of her relationship with her mother-in-law, she said, "It changed for a while when *her* daughter got pregnant with her first child, at the same time that I was pregnant with my third child. My sister-in-law acted as if I were competing for her mother's attention, which was not the case. I knew that, obviously, my mother-in-law would take her side because, after all, she was her daughter." But Lea also acknowledges that her mother-in-law tries to make things work and gives her credit for being aware of the importance of helping the relationship to stay emotionally open and supportive.

Number One: Wife or Mother?

When a son marries, the role his mother plays in his life changes. She moves from being the Number One woman to a less prominent position. If she acknowledges that her daughter-in-law is now the leading lady in her son's life, and the daughter-in-law appreciates the fact that her mother-in-law was the leading lady before her, this allows both women to empathize with the other's position. If his mother accepts this change as a natural passage and gracefully hands over the throne, saying, in effect, "You are 'Number One' in his life now," this can go a long way toward creating an amicable relationship.

Elaine, who had a very positive relationship with her own mother-in-law and now has four sons and four grandchildren of her own, put it this way: "I accept the fact that I am not the most important woman in my sons' lives. Every mother must understand that with each generation, her central role in her child's life moves farther away. In some ways we become more important, in others, less." Unfortunately, not all mothers accept their sons' growth and separation with such aplomb.

Daughters-in-law who find themselves competing with their mothers-in-law for positions of power in the family, or for attention or acknowledgement by the husband/son will often turn to their husbands for support. Then, their husbands may feel caught in the middle between the two women they love, and they will not want to choose sides. But a son/husband cannot ever be "even-handed." If he tries to be neutral, he may create a situation in which everyone feels betrayed, especially his wife, since she was selected to share his life and may now feel like an outsider.

According to Gottman and Silver (1999), one of the fundamental tasks in a marriage is "to establish a sense of 'we-ness' between husband and wife." "We-ness," as the name implies, is the bond between husband and wife that includes the two of them and them alone; it is symbolic of the unity and solidarity between the partners. "We-ness" also creates the experience of safety in a relationship.

Gottman and Silver state that, when conflict between a wife and a mother-in-law occurs, there is "only one way out," and only one choice for the husband. He *must* side with his wife. This makes the boundaries clear to everyone and, although his mother may be hurt, she'll get over it. Resolving a conflict in this way can set an invaluable precedent that may lead to a more comfortable relationship between the two women once their roles have been established.

A son who makes it clear that he cannot be swayed from his place beside his wife also makes it clear to his mother that, although he loves her and his love has not diminished, his primary allegiance is to his new family. His mother should remember her own struggles as a young wife and, hopefully, she will respect his position and admire her son's strength. A daughter-in-law who does not feel threatened by her mother-in-law is more likely to be emotionally open and comfortable around her. A successful relationship between the two women who are the "kinkeepers" (the custodians of traditions of the family) can only strengthen and create a comfortable atmosphere for the whole family.

What to Expect

For many women, having a good relationship with their mothers-in-law is tantamount to having been lucky. For others, luck has nothing to do with it. Joy, a music teacher, feels that, even though she was welcomed by her husband's family, it's been hard work that turned her relationship with her mother-in-law into a good one. She believes that her own efforts as well as her mother-in-law's made her appreciate what she has. She said, "I don't think I ever gave the relationship much thought. I'm pretty sure that I had no expectations. I mean, I liked her. My in-laws had furniture that was very similar to that of my parents, and that amused me and made me feel comfortable with them. I didn't fool myself into thinking that this meant that everything would be great and that my mother-in-law would be just like my mom."

Joy's earlier interactions with boyfriends' mothers gave her an idea of what she'd find less comfortable or more desirable. "I was very relieved that my in-laws approved of us living together before marriage," she said, "I always considered myself lucky that they were so 'cool.' My husband was relatively old to be getting married, so they were happy he had found someone and they liked me. That was great for me. One of my previous boyfriends had a mother who disapproved of me, so I knew how bad it could feel to be disapproved of by my love's mother. I was grateful to be welcomed by my husband's parents. I will say that our relationship was much simpler and there was less conflict before we had children."

Joy continued, "I think my mother-in-law and I have a good relationship. We both worked hard to make it so. I have always gone to her with my complaints and concerns, and if I had not, I am pretty sure that I wouldn't be able to love her as I do. I appreciate a lot of things about her, and I also get annoyed with some things about her. I think that, basically, she has some respect for me. But I also know that she thinks I am misguided and confused and wrong about a lot of things, usually things that are different from how she was brought up herself. She told me recently that she would give me an A minus as a parent.

"She also told me that I was doing things 99 percent right, I think. Maybe she said 90 percent. Interesting, huh? I think she feels lucky to have a daughter-in-law like me, though I think she wishes I were more like her. We are able to laugh and enjoy our conversations fairly often. But she does a lot to keep the peace. She told me once that she has learned a lot from me. Another time she told me to 'remember where my husband came from.' That was one of the most helpful things she ever said to me, as far as marital advice goes. I have always remembered that, and I am grateful to have a mother-in-law who had the intelligence to tell me that, although if I reminded her of it today, the chances are, nine out of ten, she would not remember having said it."

Common Ground

Nadja, who runs an ad agency with her husband in New York City, also didn't have a clear idea about what she should expect. "I really had no expectations. My husband had a great relationship with his mother and I loved him very much. She was a good mother to him, so I assumed that everything would be good." The warmth she received when she was accepted into the family is what Nadja noted as one of the best things about her relationship with her mother-in-law. "My mother-in-law was very inviting and welcoming from the very beginning," said Nadja, "I was asked up to my in-laws' home in Connecticut for a family dinner when we first met. She made me feel at home. It was wonderful."

It is important to be realistic about the mother-in-law/daughter-in-law relationship. Expectations for perfection will always create disappointment. Anyone going into a relationship must take into account the need to make some accommodations. For some, greater adjustments may be in order. For others, the transition may come as second nature. In general, the more different a person is from another, the more accommodations may have to be made.

This doesn't mean that "different" need be racial, ethnic, religious, or class-related. Two people raised in Catholic families, even living next door to each other, can experience two vastly different upbringings. One family may have a very reserved style of communication and the other may be fiery and temperamental. One family may have very critical, intimidating parents while the other may have parents who are openly affectionate and generous with praise. For the children raised in either house, these differences will create two very different methods of connecting and communicating. Nevertheless, close cultural ties do make for easier transitions.

Daughter-in-law, Nel, for example, was raised in a Conservative Jewish household, and married a Conservative Jewish man who was also raised in a Conservative Jewish household. She and her mother-in-law share a great deal during holidays and other religious events. It is clear, however, that common ground alone does not ensure a perfect union. Other kinds of differences can cause disharmony. Moreover, people from totally dissimilar backgrounds can learn to cherish their differences.

Luzi, an established writer, found that although she and her mother-in-law came from very different places (Luzi was raised in a large city and her mother-in-law was brought up in a small town and then raised her own children in the country), and they have very different ethnic backgrounds, they had much to share. They are both practicing Catholics and attend church faithfully. After almost thirty years of marriage, Luzi's relationship with her mother-in-law is stronger than ever. From the beginning, however, Luzi made clear her desire for her mother-in-law and herself to be like blood kin. "I have always called my mother-in-law 'mama,' " she said. "This distinguishes her from my own mother, whom I call 'ma.' I am the only one of her daughters-in-law to do so. I also believe that my mother-in-law has always liked my using that familiar term of endearment. When both of my kids were born, my mother-in-law flew out to be with me. She stayed two weeks each time and literally showed me how to take care of them."

Luzi is realistic about her mother-in-law and does not expect perfection. "Her attitude is that she raised her children and now it's up to them to live their own lives while she goes about enjoying hers. I do believe she puts *herself* first . . . and, as far as I'm concerned, that's as it should be. She rarely whines or complains. She does drop subtle hints that she would like to see the kids more often, but would never dream of inviting herself out here. She will wait for us to do so. Truth is, if she died tomorrow (God forbid), I would chastise myself for not seeing her more often."

Luzi noted that, for her, marriage brought an all-encompassing "beautiful family." "They aren't just 'in-laws,' my mother-in-law and my mother (both widows) get along very well and have done so since they first met at my wedding. In fact, they are like girlfriends. When my mother-in-law comes to visit, she stays with my mom in her big house because we don't really have the room here. She and my mom do many things together. They go shopping, to Mass, out to dinner, get their hair done *together*. This is great because when my mother-in-law is in town, my mother does a lot of the entertaining, allowing me to go about my business."

Personality Issues

Although religious differences and cultural differences are a common source of friction, their absence does not ensure harmony. Personality, views on affection, criticism, personal habits, and life choices are all integral to the formation of a daughter-in-law's relationship with her mother-in-law.

For example, Jeri's mother-in-law has found Eastern philosophies more to her liking than the Methodist church in which both she and Jeri were raised. "She is a strong-willed woman," Jeri, a copyeditor, explained. "I get along with her so long as she doesn't try to make me agree with her opinions. She is a very opinionated person and sometimes tries to make you see her view as the only right one. One time she overstepped her bounds in my home and my husband had to mediate a truce. I don't remember the specifics other than I said something like, 'This is my house,' and then she stormed out. It took about a week before things were resolved, and I think that we both forgave each other for my husband's sake."

Jeri's husband did not try to persuade his wife to yield to her mother-in-law and they both made it clear that Jeri was the woman of the house. "My husband and mother-in-law are rather close. He was the one boy who was not always at odds with her while growing up. He usually can remind her that hers is not the only view in the world. He is very even tempered with her. She can get herself worked up about things."

In spite of these issues, Jeri feels that her relationship with her mother-in-law works. "All things considered," she said, "we get along very well 99 percent of the time." She found that being open about emotional issues with her mother-in-law helped to make their relationship work. "My husband felt that it was his job to look after his mother after his father died. On several occasions, she and I talked about this attitude my husband has about feeling responsible for her, and I believe that helped make us feel more equal in our relationship."

Having a strong-willed woman around has not been a bad thing. Jeri and her mother-in-law created a relationship based on independence and mutual respect, and this works for them. "I admire her for the person she is," said Jeri, "I think we have a pretty good relationship. We communicate well and she knows that I am in charge of my life and that she can voice her opinion but I won't necessarily follow it."

Great Expectations

Expectations of what a mother-in-law/daughter-in-law relationship *should* be can be a hindrance to developing a healthy one. Having an agenda and expecting anyone to behave in a particular way will often lead to disappointment.

If, for example, a daughter-in-law expects her relationship with her mother-in-law to be intimate and loving, but the mother-in-law is not inclined to behave that way, this may be a recipe for heartache.

"I didn't know what to expect," said Emma, who married in her early twenties while her husband was getting a degree in architecture, "and I certainly don't know what my mother-in-law expected from me." When they first met, Emma and her mother-in-law really hit it off. "It was love at first sight," she said. Although her mother-in-law was living in Europe at the time, they often wrote to each other and shared much of their lives. "My mother-in-law and I got along so well when Nick and I were dating. We were fast friends. Then, suddenly, the minute we decided to get married, everything got weird."

Around the time of the wedding, Emma felt lost and overwhelmed. She turned to her mother-in-law for guidance, but she did not receive the support she needed and had hoped for. "My mother-in-law told me how it was going to be. She said her son was always going to be her son, and she hoped that I didn't expect to suddenly become a part of the family just because I was marrying him. I hadn't expected anything," Emma said, "but I certainly didn't expect that."

Feeling hurt, Emma withdrew from any further intimacy. Her mother-in-law became even less supportive and, in turn, Emma became more uncomfortable and insecure. During the wedding, her mother-in law was courteous but nothing more. Emma felt that she had been rejected, suddenly without warning. She also felt that her mother-in-law was judging her by mysterious criteria. "I didn't know what she wanted from me or how to act without inspiring a negative reaction. I was really devastated."

After the wedding, her mother-in-law tried to apologize for being so distant. Her explanation was that she had never wanted to be thought of as a mother-in-law. Emma said, "But she was a mother-in-law, I mean, what was that all about? I felt like she was suddenly acting like the stereotypical mother-in-law from all the jokes. How could I forgive her? I almost canceled my wedding because of her. The truth is that now we get along great. We are both strong-willed women and needed time to find our footing."

Mariette, an interior decorator, noted that, although many of her mother-in-law's actions were unforgivable, she found a way to move past them. "We've finally become friends," she said. "My family is now a group that my mother-in-law wants to be a part of. Before that, she felt she was in competition with me for her son's affection."

Before meeting her mother-in-law to-be, Mariette had hoped for a warm relationship, but "It was clear from the start that my mother-in-law and I would not get along famously. Before I met her, I imagined that my mother-in-law would be like a second mother or a loving aunt to me." But that was not to be. "My husband and I joke that if you combined my somewhat distant and uninvolved parents with his very involved, controlling mom we would have 'normal parents,'" laughed Mariette.

"My parents were quite controlling when I was growing up but they relaxed quite a bit (maybe too much!) as I got older. My husband spent much of his childhood with his somewhat distant father and his very warm stepmother. One thing that complicated my relationship with my mother-in-law is that my husband's stepmother and I get along so well. My mother-in-law was always very jealous of my husband's stepmother and stepsisters. My husband's stepfamily is quite large and they accepted me right away. I met them about a year after meeting my mother-in-law and I was very grateful not to be shunned."

Marrying the Family

An age-old adage that states "You're not marrying the family" is, simply, a fallacy. Since we are all products of our families, whether we are like them or rebel against them, our families are a part of us. Often a woman will have second thoughts about marrying a man whose family she finds unbearable. Conversely, there are marriages that remain intact because of the love shared between mother-in-law and daughter-in-law.

"Before I met my husband," said Judith, who is an X-ray technician during the day and an enthusiastic photographer in her free time. "I lived with a man for two years and I *really* didn't like his parents. I knew that I could never marry him because the thought of spending my life with such in-laws was truly unthinkable. I had no image of what the perfect in-laws would look like, but I hoped they would be as much as possible like my parents, which was pretty much how it turned out. My parents and in-laws are quite similar (with some important differences). Nowadays, we are developing a tradition of all of us having Thanksgiving at my parents' house—and Passover seder at my in-laws'. Judith noted that, although her relationship with her mother-in-law isn't perfect, there is room to grow. "We're very warm with each other. In many, many ways, she's the ideal mother-in-law. She's very supportive of the things I do. When I had a photographic exhibit recently, she came with a rose in hand and bought one of my landscapes. It made me feel great."

The Line in the Sand

It is imperative to determine boundaries between wife, spouse, and mother-in-law. If the mother-in-law is never told that when she imposes in certain ways, it is uncomfortable for others, how can she know she is doing anything wrong? It can be difficult for a daughter-in-law to make a stand for her place as Number One in her husband's life in his mother's view. Sometimes the difficulty arises because it is hard for the couple to know when and where to draw the line.

"For a while," Judith said, "when my husband and I first moved in together, my mother-in-law called us at least once a day, sometimes more than once a day, each time with a question more ridiculous than the last one. It seemed as though she couldn't help herself—as if the phone were actually an intercom and we were living in an adjoining room. One time she called in the middle of the day (I work at home), to ask if we had recently washed our car. She thought the car had looked impressively shiny when she drove by the house and she wanted to know. A few weeks ago, she phoned my husband at his office to tell him that IKEA had opened a store near us. I only get a little annoyed with these calls. But my husband really gets angry, He yells at her over the phone, 'Whose mother calls them at work???'"

Although it is important to draw clear lines, it is also important to understand that your mother-in-law may not be behaving arbitrarily or making empty demands. Look deeper and consider whether she may be in need of some further connection with you and her son. Although you must take care of your own needs, you must also make room for your mother-in-law. Judith is learning to address privacy issues. She wants to move out of the "adjoining room" and create a more mutually agreeable level of contact. She is in the formative stages of her marriage and just finding her footing.

Quantity of contact may, in fact, be the repetitive pursuit of quality of contact. A mother-in-law's apparently excessive demands may be her way of asking for something she doesn't feel she is getting. She may call more often than you like because the contact she does have with you and/or your husband lacks something.

Judith said that she thinks much of the difficulty she has with her mother-in-law comes from the newness of their relationship. Sometimes she experiences her mother-in-law as intrusive, but she knows that her husband's mother is really kind and wants to be helpful. Occasionally, though, she feels manipulated by her mother-in-law. "When my husband tries to put the brakes on, she pouts and lays on the guilt. He's very receptive to the guilt trip. So am I, it turns out—which has been the biggest surprise of this whole relationship. I *do* care what she thinks. And I don't want to seem ungrateful for her generosity. Just in the last year, she and my father-in-law paid for half our wedding, helped us buy a car, and gave us a gift of stock. They've often bought groceries for us, too. I want to be grateful for their gifts—so it feels bad to also want space."

Marking the Boundaries

June was a self-employed gardener for fifteen years. She recently married for the first time at the age of thirty-eight, and she also experienced her mother-in-law's phone calls and requests for visits as intrusive early on in their relationship. "I found it hard to demarcate boundaries with my mother-in-law," June said. "It felt artificial to, all of a sudden, have this phone connection with someone I barely knew. I knew that, for her, I was instant family and she wanted to develop a real relationship. But for me, that early in my marriage, it definitely felt like 'three's a crowd' when she would beg us for more frequent visits.

"In any case, I found myself delaying before calling her back. At one point, I gingerly confronted her. I told her how hard it is to tear myself away from my husband. I explained that it was hard to carve out time for anything else. In the context of being newlyweds, this was really understandable. In truth, my reluctance was not just with her. I really am enthralled with my husband and I try to protect what little time we have together. Liam is a botanist at the university and I have at least three big landscaping projects a month. It is so hard to ever find time to be together. I thought that if I laid it out that way, not blaming her or judging her needs, but emphasizing my absorption with her son, that she would understand where I was coming from." June's mother-in-law was charmed by her daughter-in-law's explanation and she gave the newlyweds more space.

Boundary Lines and Proximity

When Estelle, a kindergarten teacher, and her husband, a programmer, decided to buy a house, she knew that negotiating satisfactory boundaries would be a difficult task. She had been ambivalent about living near her mother-in-law, but she also wanted to be there if she or her husband were ever needed. "The in-laws live just a few miles away from us," she said. "When we started looking for a house, I was adamantly against looking in their area for months and months. Eventually, we found a neighborhood near them that seemed satisfactory. I was worried that the close proximity would result in unexpected visits, but they don't do that."

"If anything, being close by has made it easier for my husband to stop over there when a light fixture breaks or they need help with the awnings. Considering the short distance, I don't see my in-laws that often. We get together on holidays and my husband's whole family spends a week at the beach every year vacationing together. Other than that, there are occasional visits, or we'll stop by there if they need something. My husband talks to his mother about once a week. Sometimes I'm in the room for their conversations (we have a speaker phone), other times not."

However, Estelle finds herself uncomfortable spending time with her mother-in-law. "She is extremely inquisitive, bordering on nosy, and that bothers me. I think she's extremely interested in her children's lives because she doesn't have many outside interests. But at times it's too much for me. For instance, she met a few of my friends at social events. Ever since then she constantly asks about them, their families, their jobs, their prospects, and so on and so on. All this in addition to wanting all the details about whatever my husband and I are doing. Then, she gets insulted when I clam up and stop answering. Don't get me wrong, she is a very sweet woman. She just has a need to know everything about everyone and I find that very hard to take."

Feedback and Boundary Lines

Nadja feels fortunate. Her mother-in-law not only welcomed her new daughter-in-law into her family, she became good friends with Nadja's mother. In spite of the good relationship they have, Nadja said that communication between the two of them certainly could be better. She knows that she doesn't get enough feedback from her mother-in-law. Nadja often feels that she may have hurt her mother-in-law's feelings and never knows why. She believes that her mother-in-law doesn't tell her how she really feels about things.

Nadja said, "To her credit, she doesn't interfere. I am extremely independent and though she respects my choices she does not always agree. Most times she says nothing, and sometimes it takes years for me to find out how she really felt about an issue or event."

Nadja described her marriage ceremony as an example of the lack of feedback from her mother-in-law. "My husband and I decided to get married after living together for five years in our jointly owned home. One weekend we decided to get married the following Friday. We chose to get married at City Hall with just my parents, my in-laws, and my brother-in-law in attendance. We went to my in-laws' house after the ceremony and then later that evening to a nice restaurant. My mother-in-law invited some close relatives to visit her house before we went out to dinner. Although we had not known she was going to do that, we were glad to see them. I thought that everyone enjoyed the day, including the dinner.

"Years later, when my mother-in-law was talking about an upcoming wedding, I found out that although she had been thrilled that my husband and I got married, and though the day was lovely, she was very hurt and disappointed that she never had the opportunity to have all of the relatives share in the day. She would have liked to have given a party for us. I had never known that was how she felt. I'm not sure I would have done anything differently, but she never said a word about being so disappointed. Anyway, despite her disappointment she has always been great to us."

Second-Chance Family

Women who long for intimacy with their own mothers may find intimacy in their relationships with their mothers-in-law. For some women whose relationships with their own mothers were difficult or unfulfilling, a mother-in-law can become the mother they never had. Craving such a connection, a daughter-in-law might place unfair expectations on a less receptive mother-in-law. But if a mother-in-law also wants an intimate relationship with her daughter-in-law, or is looking for the daughter she never had, this can become a very rewarding relationship.

Some women have relationships with their mothers-in-law that are stronger and closer than their relationships with their own mother. According to Helene Arnstein (1985), parents-in-law may provide a "second-chance family" for some women. For example, Larrissa said that although she had not expected to become intimate with her mother-in-law, she did like her from the very beginning. "I actually can't remember the first time I met her. I do recall thinking she was a very warm, affectionate person. But I certainly didn't expect our relationship to be so close. And I never expected that we would be even closer than my relationship with my own mother."

Larrissa, a college teacher who lives in western Canada, was never very intimate with her mother. "My parents were in the Peace Corps. I was brought up as an only child in a variety of developing countries, relocating every few years. My husband, Jim, on the other hand, spent the first eighteen years of his life in the same house. He is the youngest of eight and they are all close. Jim is the adored baby of the family. I never had that kind of affection."

Meeting her husband's family and finding the warmth and embracing presence of his mother so inviting, Larrissa feels that she now has the family she never had. "I think Joan would say she considers me a daughter. In many ways, I am more comfortable around her than around my own mother. I find her much easier to confide in and talk to than my own mother. She's also much more affectionate with me than my own mother is. My mom was always a bit awkward as a mother, anyway. I don't blame her that she doesn't participate in certain things." Clearly, Larrissa's mother-in-law, Joan, handles the maternal role with greater ease than her mother.

Larrissa said, "Joan, who is adored by all of her children and in-law children, is really a natural. Plus, I feel the two of us share something special. My mother-in-law took me shopping for my wedding dress, which is something most brides do with their actual mothers, I believe. She insisted on doing it once she found out that my own mom wasn't going to. Joan bought me an absolutely exquisite, and very expensive, dress and we spent the entire day together. It was such a pleasure. We both thoroughly enjoyed every second of that day. When our baby was born, Joan flew from Toronto to Vancouver immediately, foregoing her own Christmas plans. She spent two weeks with us and was amazingly supportive, helping us with everything from laundry to coaching me while I was breast-feeding. My mother would never have done that. I don't blame her, but I am so glad I had Joan. It makes me sad that we are on opposite ends of the country. I'd like to live within driving distance of her!"

This intimacy between daughter-in-law and mother-in-law has not been without friction. Larrissa's own mother has felt displaced, and there has been some discomfort as a result. Larrissa said, "Our fathers are very much alike and enjoy one another's company. Our mothers' relationship is not so great. My mother is insecure around Joan and feels threatened by her, perhaps because I clearly like Joan so much. My mother was also offended a long time ago by some well-meaning things that Joan did and she has held a grudge ever since."

Creating her own family with her husband has also been a bit of a challenge because Larrissa feels that her mother-in-law set an impossible standard. She also knows that she married mama's little baby. "Can anyone say 'spoiled'?" she asked. "My husband was totally coddled. I was a bit worried that my mother-in-law assumed I would follow suit and that I was expected to take on the doting role of caregiver for Jim. Put it this way, Joan used to put Jim's pajamas in the dryer every night so they'd be warm when he put them on at bedtime . . . need I say more?"

Eva, who is a child advocate and minority activist in Washington, D.C., also has found that her relationship with her mother-in-law is more natural and nurturing than with her own mother. She said, "I get along with my mother-in-law better than with my own mom, I'm sorry to say. At first, I was very concerned whether my in-laws would accept me at all, much less *like* me. I am African-American and my husband and his family are all Caucasians. When this seemed to not make a difference, I assumed my relationship with my mother-in-law would be either strained or like my relationship with my mom. Respect, manners, and etiquette are of the utmost importance to my mother. This creates a lot of distance between us.

"When Jason and I were dating, he had to call my mom 'Mrs. Grantley,' while I called his 'Claire.' He didn't call my mother by her first name until after we were married, and we dated for five years! When we were ready to marry, Jason asked my mother's permission. I think she would have been dismayed if he had not.

"To me, my mother-in-law, Claire, represents the epitome of motherhood. The first Christmas I spent with her, she had seventeen presents waiting for me when I arrived, and she cried when I left. I love my mother, but when I got to know Claire, I felt that she was the dream mother and the kind of mother I wanted to be."

Eva has managed to keep her "two mothers" separate and she has not allowed friction to develop between them. Eva pointed out that, "Claire had Jason when she was eighteen so they have a more 'generational' tie. Also, Claire is very open in her discussions with her children. They can talk to her about 'anything.' My mom had me at the age of thirty-four. I know that age alone doesn't build a wall, but we have a real generation gap between us. I don't speak until I'm spoken to. I don't discuss controversial issues with her. She wouldn't want to, first of all, and I also believe that she would simply disagree with whatever I thought. In my mother's house the adage 'Children should be seen and not heard' was the rule. In Jason's, it wasn't. Recently, Jason, the kids, and I moved to D.C. from Delaware, three hours from both of our families. Claire will drive down and see us at least once a month and, if asked, she will visit at the drop of a hat. My mother has yet to come for a visit. I would never feel comfortable pointing this out to her. We don't have the kind of relationship where I'd feel confident doing that. But I would never tell her that my mother-in-law does come to visit. That way she won't be jealous of Claire.

Daughter/Mentor/Friend

Although there are mother-in-law and daughter-in-law relationships as close as some mother/daughter relationships, there is something unique about the type of intimacy between mother and child. In Duvall's 1954 study of in-laws, she noted that 15.9 percent of the women respondents said that their mother-in-law was *like* a mother to them. But certain behavior patterns or habits of familiarity can have a negative effect on a mother/ daughter relationship. Some bonds, true unconditional familial bonds, can permit a certain amount of disrespect or poor behavior because the connection is never at risk. The maternal type of bond that can take place between mother-in-law and daughter-in-law is generally free of the family "baggage" and emotional trespasses, while still allowing for intimacy.

Nel credits her mother-in-law for helping her to develop the strength to cope with her own family problems. "I went eight years without speaking to my father after many years of difficulties with him. Throughout the rift, my mother-in-law supported my decision not to reconnect with my father. She said I needed to do whatever was right for me and my growing family." Having someone there to support her, someone who was both part and not part of her family, was important to Nel and helped her find the strength to stand firm in her decision. "She told me how proud she was of me for going there alone and facing an uncomfortable situation with dignity. I told her that she had helped me to reach that point in my life. We were both sobbing together on the phone. In the years since, I have resumed my relationship with my father, and my mother-in-law has, once again, supported my decision."

Barbara Quick (2000) has written about women's needs for same-sex mentors. She says, "The distinction between good mother and good mentoring" was not absolutely clear for many of the women she interviewed. She also found that many of the women who had mentors not related by blood believed that they had been "inadequately mothered the first time around." This fits with Arnstein's theory of "second-chance families." Nel found both mentor and mother in her mother-in-law. "My mother-in-law is one of the best friends I have ever had. She has played a huge role in my becoming who I am. I have known her since I was twenty-one years old and she has always been an excellent role model." Unfortunately, this sentiment has led to some awkwardness in Nel's relationship with her own mother.

What does it mean to have a "second-chance family" when your "first-chance family" is alive and well? For Nel, her mother felt displaced. "There were difficult moments in the early years because my mother was very threatened by my relationship with my husband's mother. Nowadays, my mother has come around a bit and accepts the fact that I can love both her and my mother-in-law."

Summary Questions

Reading this book, as well as gathering information from other sources, will provide you with insights about your relationship with your mother-in-law. These insights will not be change agents in and of themselves. But they may lead you to emotional engagement and actions toward effecting real change and growth.

Now, take a deep breath. Create a comfortable, quiet place to answer the following questions. These questions are meant to generate open and honest reflection, heighten your emotional awareness, and guide you toward deeper insight about your relationship with your mother-in-law. They are designed to help you to create a new direction by encouraging you to investigate conditions you may not have considered before.

You may find it useful to answer your questions in your journal or in a separate notebook that you keep for this purpose. By the time you finish answering all of the questions in this book, you may find that some of your feelings and thoughts about your mother-in-law have changed, and you will then have a written record of how that came about.

❋ *How would you describe your relationship with your mother-in-law? Good/Bad/Ugly? Are there any particular events or issues that illustrate why you feel this way? Can you describe those events or issues?*

❋ *How would you describe the relationship dynamics between your mother-in-law/husband/yourself?*

❋ *How would you describe your relationship with your mother?*

Chapter 2

How Good Is Good?

There's another kind of energy, besides the need to be giving. I find her very needy, which makes me suspicious (and sometimes resentful) of her doting. Sometimes, I feel that her kindness is meant to force reciprocal attention. She'll call up and say, "I made your favorite kind of soup." And we will say, "We have plans tonight and tomorrow night and we can't get there." She'll answer, "I'll come by and drop it off."

—Judith

She has been great in so many ways and very helpful to me. I have to give her credit for helping me learn how to take initiatives with my children that I would not have learned without her guidance, such as with toilet training.

—Joy

When we ask the question, "What is "good"? we also need to ask, "How good is good?" Sometimes, a relationship really is good if everyone is content, even if the circumstances seem difficult or awkward. For example, if your mother-in-law lives thousands of miles away from you and you think your relationship works, then it works. If your mother-in-law lives in your house and you have close, daily, contact and you both think it works, then it works. If it is acceptable, then it is acceptable. If it only *seems* acceptable, then you must ask, is it *really* acceptable? The daughter-in-law must honestly evaluate the situation as it looks to her.

Is Good Always Good?

Many of the daughters-in-law we surveyed who reported having "good" relationships also had serious areas of conflict and difficulty with particular traits of their mothers-in-law. They were, however, able to negotiate these issues. Clearly, no relationship is without its imperfections, no matter how wonderful it is. Being able to progress from the earliest stage and to grow and change through many years into something comfortable, intimately familiar, intense, or profound is usually agreed upon as good. Some new relationships hold promise, others have less of a chance of thriving because of various factors.

When people are unwilling or unable to communicate, or the needs of one person do not match those of the other, difficulties loom large. Although Judith finds her mother-in-law kind, she doesn't believe that it is always pure altruism that motivates her husband's mother. "There's often an undercurrent to her affection," said Judith, who is an X-ray technician, "There's another kind of energy, besides the need to be giving. I find her very needy, which makes me suspicious (and sometimes resentful) of her doting. Sometimes, I feel that her kindness is meant to force reciprocal attention. She'll call up and say, 'I made your favorite kind of soup.' And we will say, 'We have plans tonight and tomorrow night and we can't get there.' She'll answer, 'I'll come by and drop it off.'"

This behavior clearly feels intrusive to Judith. She acknowledges that she isn't used to someone doting on her the way her mother-in-law does. But, although her mother-in-law does cause her to feel uncomfortable by trying to insert herself into the newlyweds' life, Judith also believes that everyone will eventually figure out their space without always stepping on each others' toes, and that matters can only improve with time. "Don't get me wrong, things are good, and they can always get better."

Joy, the music teacher, also has had to negotiate some uncomfortable interactions with her mother-in-law. "Once, when my eldest daughter, who is now nine, was about two years old, my mother-in-law was giving her a bath. I was rehearsing in the next room. When it was time to get Imogene out of the tub, I heard my mother-in-law tell her that she would go down the drain if she didn't get out of the tub. She was using fear as a manipulation tactic. She wanted to scare Imogene into doing what she wanted and wasn't thinking of the impact it had on my daughter, I guess.

"Anyhow, at the time I guess I didn't say anything. But the next time I was going to give Imogene a bath, she was afraid to get in the tub because she was convinced she would be sucked down the drain. I told her she wouldn't but, of course, Imogene had trusted what her grandmother said. Right then and there, I called up my mother-in-law and told her that Imogene was freaked out about taking baths because she had been frightened. I explained to my mother-in-law what I thought had transpired between them the last time she had given her granddaughter a bath.

"At first, she denied saying any such thing, but I told her I had overheard what she had said. She was silent for a moment and, then, I think she remembered the event and what she had said. She had intended no harm and I think she was genuinely devastated that she had caused her grand-daughter any distress. I asked her to please get on the phone with Imogene and tell her that it wasn't true that she would or could go down the drain. My mother-in-law did as I requested, and I was so relieved, and my daughter was able to approach the tub with less fear.

"Then," Joy continued, "the following year, my mother-in-law, told my three-year-old daughter, Veronica, that *she* would go down the drain if she didn't get out of the tub immediately. Veronica knew better, thankfully so. When she informed me of this event, I simply told her that some-times her 'nana' says goofy things. It made me mad to hear that my mother-in-law made the same 'stupid mistake' (in my judgment), but I wasn't very surprised. Long-standing behaviors can be very hard to change.

"I really do believe there was no malice or cruelty involved in either of these events. I think my mother-in-law thought she was being funny, or it was just her way of manipulating the kids. She has been great in so many ways and very helpful to me. I have to give her credit for helping me learn how to take initiatives with my children that I would not have learned without her guidance, such as with toilet training. I was too deferential with my son until I learned what she taught me so well: how to guide."

Acknowledging Differences

Joy knows that a *good* relationship means working at it. It doesn't mean that things are easy by any means. Successful conflict resolution can be good in itself. The testimony to a good relationship can be seen in how two very different peo-ple get along so successfully. "My mother-in-law has so much to offer. We're very different but I appreciate her, I really do. What I both appreciate and struggle with is that my mother-in-law is strong-minded and outspoken. What I do not like about her is that she acts too bossy, judgmental, and presumptuous sometimes, and she is not very self-aware. Given when and where she grew up, and her life experience, however, I think that, generally, she is quite a wonderful woman. I feel lucky to have her as my mother-in-law."

"I also know that our relationship would have suffered terribly if I had not chosen to be open with her about my occasional bad feelings about her. I'm glad I had a mother who allowed me to express myself and did not judge me for it. Having been open and communicative with my mother-in-law has allowed the good to outweigh the bad in the total scheme of things."

Although Joy describes her relationship with her mother-in-law as "good," clearly there have been some difficulties and emotional strains throughout their years of relating to each other. Joy believes that disclosure and communication are vital aspects of a good relationship. She has found that actions speak louder than words and that her mother-in-law would, perhaps, like fewer words than Joy likes to share. "Once my mother-in-law told me to come to her if I ever had a problem, or something like that," she remembers. "I took that to mean that if I ever had a problem with her, it would be okay for me to go to her. But the first time I did that, it was clear that that wasn't what she had meant. We managed, however, and repeated the process again and again."

For some daughters-in-law, the need to have an intimate relationship with their mothers-in-law is either not pressing or, for some, apparently not even present. Lahna, who publishes a successful, award-winning magazine and has a history in graphic arts, said she is very happy with her relationship with her mother-in-law. When they first met, she thought she was "cool." "They [in-laws] were young compared to my parents. They rode a motorcycle, a Harley. I felt that Mark's mom was pretty cool to do that."

Lahna does not live near her in-laws so there is no day-to-day contact. In fact, they speak on the phone about once a month and the conversation often does not go beyond small talk. "The fact that my mother-in-law steered clear of certain topics of conversation is a testimony to the strength of our relationship. I believe she respects my opinions." However, Lahna admitted that if there was more intimate contact, the differences between the two of them could make things more difficult. So for Lahna, avoiding difficult subjects and retaining a comfortable distance seems to work well. Lahna has never felt any discomfort or stress between her spouse and herself in relation to her mother-in-law.

Mariette has shown great magnanimity toward her mother-in-law, the woman who had rejected her in such an ugly way (see chapters 1 and 9). Instead of rejecting her mother-in-law, Mariette chose to understand her. She explained that she saw her mother-in-law's cruelty as a symptom of her insecurity. "I wish I could find a way to assure my mother-in-law that I (and of course my husband) love her and will never abandon her. Perhaps she would be less demanding and needy if she knew that." The strong bond Mariette shares with her husband kept her from ever feeling that her mother-in-law's behavior was a danger to her marriage. Now her relationship with her mother-in-law is good, and she feels it is so because she made it clear, as did her husband, that no one could ever come between them.

Although they are close now, Emma and her mother-in-law spent several difficult years barely speaking. She did not feel that she had her husband, Nick's, active support, although she knew that his heart was with her. Emma, like Mariette, felt rejected by her mother-in-law and, like Mariette, chose to avoid her as much as possible. But her mother-in-law also chose to stay away and Emma saw this as further proof of rejection. "I was convinced my mother-in-law hated me and, although my husband and I were a strong team and very much in love, I felt that she didn't give me any credit for being a supportive partner."

Emma's husband, Nick, felt that he was caught in the middle and chose to ignore the situation. He felt that his relationship with his parents was fragile and he feared that expressing anything contrary to their wishes might rupture the delicate balance. Emma never expressed how awkward she felt when she was excluded from his family's gatherings.

"He'd say, 'Are you sure it's all right if I go to one of Dad's performances without you?' Nick's dad is a concert violinist and Nick was invited to attend his performances and I was not. There was no acknowledgment that he and I were partners. But I would never dream of saying, 'Hey, don't you think that it's uncool to invite one spouse and not the other?' It's not like it's a special time for togetherness. It's a public performance and I was clearly not wanted. I wasn't even given the choice. If Nick didn't see that, I wasn't going to say anything."

The problem here was that, although it was not a good time in her relationship with her mother-in-law, it was made worse by her husband's lack of sensitivity. Had Nick expressed concern or chosen not to attend his father's concerts, he would have made it clear that he was not going to collude in his wife's exclusion.

It is vital to a good spousal relationship that the allegiance between husband and wife is the primary allegiance. Anything that appears to threaten this bond creates friction and difficulties and can have potentially devastating effects on a marriage. But Emma and Nick worked on their marriage and were able to rediscover each other and rebuild what they had begun. "Now I realize that my mother-in-law was doing the same thing I was: trying to avoid uncomfortable interactions. She thought she was giving me space. I didn't actually want to be around on all these events and trips. If we weren't getting along, why force the situation?" This also applied to family gatherings.

At first, when Emma began to be invited to join Nick's family, she wanted to say, "Forget it, you rejected me and now I don't want you." But she didn't. She realized this would only make matters even more uncomfortable. She and Nick discussed her feelings and he saw what he had been doing to contribute to her alienation. He understood that in their new marriage, he was sending her a message that said he was a part of a different family, one from which she was excluded. Then, "My mother-in-law and I began to see each other occasionally, then more often. I began to understand how awkward and unnatural it must be being a mother-in-law. I tried to really watch my own behavior. Was I rejecting her? I realized that I was lucky not to be forced into attending every single family event. I guess it was just important to know that Nick was with me and not party to excluding me."

Nick found that his fears about rupturing his bond with his parents were unfounded. By bringing their difficulties out in the open and discussing the issues that were plaguing Emma, everyone benefited from the honesty. Nevertheless, it is important to note here that full disclosure can bring about a climate of confrontation and create new problems. Sensitivity to everyone's position is essential to achieving good results.

Emma is acutely aware of this: "Had I confronted Nick or my mother-in-law early on, I might have made a terrible mess of things," she admitted. "By waiting until I had really given it some thought, really considered what my needs were, and what kind of outcome I hoped to achieve, I feel as if I really got the best results. It was important to tell Nick how I felt, but it was more important to know how I felt myself."

Playing an Active Role

Although Emma feels she did best by waiting until she clearly understood what her needs were, this is not the usual recipe for a successful relationship with your in-laws. The process of communicating with your husband while you are actively finding meaning in confusing feelings, and learning how to articulate those feelings, is very strengthening.

A relationship is never static, so there is no need to have a crystal clear account of how you feel before you discuss an issue. Your feelings are likely to change anyway. Trust the exploratory conversation. In addition, matters may resolve themselves in time. Emma said, "After my first daughter was born, my mother-in-law and I began to spend more time together and found that what we first saw in each other was still there. In fact, we found that we were very much alike."

Working to improve matters or to keep relations as good as they can be should be a part of any relationship. Expecting things to work out without any thought given as to how they might will not always yield the hoped-for results. Being thoughtful about your own needs, and being considerate about others' needs will help to keep things clear and help relationships to progress rather than falter. Because every relationship is different, it is also important to be clear on what works for you. Many people look at other relationships for guidance without considering what would work best in their own lives with their own circumstances.

Emma explained, "Taking trips to visit his parents when they wanted intimate time alone with their son was never an issue. In fact, there were trips that I was glad not to attend. My parents thought this was weird and they were constantly afraid for my situation. But I had watched my mother get dragged along on trips she hated. I never felt like I had to be there whenever Nick visited his family." Allowing room for personal space, and for intimacy to continue between mother and son, also may have helped take the tension out of this mother-in-law/daughter-in-law relationship. "I would hope that, when my sons get married, that my future daughters-in-law would let me have my boys all to myself once in a while."

Making Room for Good

There are innumerable reasons why relationships that seem to be good, and are considered good, are, at heart, truly problematic. A daughter-in-law may hear the overt message from her mother-in-law as positive, yet experience the latent communication as negative. A daughter-in-law may present herself as participating in a positive relationship, but when telling her story, she may realize she harbors ill feelings she had not acknowledged previously. We found many daughters-in-law initially called their relationships "good," but when they told their stories, we found that matters were not always as they had been categorized.

For example, Ellen named her mother-in-law/daughter-in-law relationship as "good," although clearly it was not the relationship she had hoped for. Initially, Ellen had been seen as the perfect daughter-in-law-to-be by her mother-in-law. "She knew I was for him and told everyone she thought so." But Ellen believed that it was her own efforts that made the relationship work.

Ellen and her husband, Philip, were very close with her parents, much closer than he had ever been with his. In fact, early in their relationship, Ellen began promoting greater involvement with his parents. She was accustomed to a close-knit family and had hopes of creating another one with the family she had married into. This attempt led to other problems. When Ellen met her mother-in-law, Ellen was attending the art institute and her mother-in-law was a fairly successful ceramist. "At first I thought it was great that we had so much in common. I thought she was funny and a bit odd. Her pottery had a unique character to it. Whimsical, I guess you could say. She was thrilled to meet me when Phil first took me to their home. She never said a negative thing about me in her life."

But the habits that Ellen found quirky soon led to disturbing revelations. "Certain behavior she exhibited made me very uncomfortable. She exaggerated or changed details about an event, even if the truth would have been just as entertaining. She is a sweet woman, but I began to find some of her habits petty and I also began to resent spending all the time with them that I had promoted in the beginning of our marriage. Philip wanted to show his family how generous he was and he invited them for dinner once a week, even against my desires. This was while I was still in school and also teaching. Philip didn't cook so the responsibility was on me."

Although Ellen considered her relationship with her mother-in-law "good," the negative impact that it had on her relationship with her husband has continued through nearly fifty years of marriage. Annoying traits of her mother-in-law that might have gone unnoticed had she and Philip been more united, were exaggerated by her own sense of insecurity. Ellen couldn't stop resenting the time her husband spent on the phone with his parents. She now realizes that her husband was trying to re-create with his parents the relationship they shared with her family. But his parents were not like Ellen's and this only fostered discord between husband and wife. The more interactions he had with his parents, the more he invited them to their home, and the more Ellen felt displaced. The unfamiliar habits of her in-laws caused her to feel strange and, hence, estranged. But she, rightly, does not blame her mother-in-law for the discord. It is important to consider all relationships surrounding a marriage when things are not feeling right.

Summary Questions

* *How do your parents and your spouse's parents get along? Why do you think this works or doesn't work?*

* *Describe your mother's relationship with her mother-in-law.*

* *Was your childhood/upbringing very different from that of your husband's?*

* *How would you characterize your husband's relationship with his mother now? In what way might this influence circumstances between you and your mother-in- law?*

Chapter 3

Your Spouse's Family

I feel that I am partly responsible for helping my husband heal his relationship with his mom, and that makes me feel good, because she leans on him more now, and I know she needs help because she is going through a tough time.

—Juanita

Recently, I unfortunately told her that if she'd had a girl, either her daughter would have killed her or vice versa. I haven't apologized yet.

—Joy

My mother-in-law encouraged me on many occasions to call her "Mom." She signs cards to me with "Mom." I call her by her first name, though. It feels phony to call her "Mom," and in some ways, disrespectful to my parents.

—Judith

We are each a product of the family from whence we came. That is just a fact. We may be different from our relatives, we may follow family patterns or rebel against them, but we are products of our families. So are our spouses products of their families. Taking a look at the families of our spouses can provide us with insight into how those family dynamics work. It is also interesting to note that certain aspects of family life tend to emerge in force when a member of that family marries.

Family Circles

Family members have their own unique way of relating to one another, dealing with issues, and communicating. When we join with someone else and begin a new family, naturally, we bring to this new relationship what we learned in our family of origin.

Juanita, a computer consultant who lives in Santa Fe, talked about her husband's family and how different it was from hers. She described how the dynamics of her husband's relations with his family changed for the better because of her efforts. "When I first met my husband, his relationship with his mother was not very good. There was a lot of anger on both sides. I think that, of all the kids in his family, my husband was the one most affected by his parents' divorce. He was seven and was very close to his dad. After the divorce, their mom remarried and moved them all to New York, far away from Phoenix and their dad. My mother-in-law says that of all her kids, my husband is the most like her, which she thinks is the reason they clashed so much during my husband's adolescence and young adulthood.

"Anyway, when we were first together, my husband would refuse to call his mom at all, even on her birthday, which seemed really wrong to me because I am very close to my own mom. I used to hassle him until he would call her because I wanted him to make things right with her. After we'd been living together a little while, we took a trip from Phoenix, where we lived, back east to Washington, D.C. His mom's home is in Manhattan, three hours away, and I convinced my husband to make the trip to visit her.

"I was really happy to see them getting along together, even though this was one of the first times I'd been around my mother-in-law and I was still somewhat uncomfortable. But she and Jordie (my husband), talked some and joked some about their relationship, and since then, they have built their relationship back up. In fact, as I write this, my husband is in New York, helping his mom out with some things around the apartment, now that his step-dad is unable to help her much anymore.

"I feel that I am partly responsible for helping my husband heal his relationship with his mom, and that makes me feel good, because she leans on him more now, and I know she needs help because she is going through a tough time. The relationship among the three of us is good now. We all respect each other and care about each other.

"Jordie and I both grew up in white, middle-class homes, so, in that sense, our backgrounds are similar, but there are some differences that I think do have some bearing on our relationship. My parents are practicing Roman Catholics and they are politically conservative. My father is from Spain. My husband's parents, natural and step, are all much more liberal. They are either atheists or agnostics, and are not as rule-bound as my parents. And, my parents are still married, where my husband's are divorced. I think my husband's family is a lot less hung up on keeping up appearances and, in general, are more tolerant of different ways of life. To my husband's family, it was no big deal when we lived together before marriage, but my own mother didn't speak to me for three months after Jordie and I moved in together."

Music teacher Joy identified the vast difference in the emotional climate within her husband's family of origin and her own and how this has had an impact on the families' values and approach to child rearing. Joy explained, "My upbringing was quite different from my husband's, emotionally, that is, not materially. We were both raised by intelligent, well-educated, politically aware, liberal parents. However, my parents were divorced and my mother raised three children alone. She had studied child psychology and she was very involved in her children's lives. She valued who I was and who I wanted to be, and gave me lots of choices. How I felt about things mattered to my mother. I felt respected by her.

"My husband and his brothers were treated very differently. My husband was told what to do all the time. There was no concern or care about his own views or about his identity. He was simply taught to 'do the right thing,' never mind how he felt. His parents wanted him to be a good person and they cared what their son did, but they didn't really take into account how that would work with who he was or what he wanted. I'm not sure how our different upbringings are ultimately important but they present challenges. We are constantly learning how to bridge the gaps."

Larrissa and her husband also come from very different families of origin. She is an only child whose parents were in the Peace Corps and they traveled a lot when Larrissa was a child. Her husband is the youngest of eight and always lived in the same house. His large family is very close and affectionate. Larrissa's family is not. Larrissa said, "My husband is very much his mother's baby and she is extremely protective and proud of him. Until this past year, I felt very uncomfortable saying anything even remotely negative about him around her. However, since the birth of our little boy, she seems more willing to criticize my husband, and to listen to my occasional complaint about him. In general, the three of us get along beautifully."

Like Larrissa, Estelle's upbringing was quite different from her husband's. "Sam is nine years older than me, he has an older sister, and his mother started late," she said. "My mother-in-law, Zoe, is eighty-two years old. To be honest, I don't know much about her background, though I know she was raised in New Haven.

"My mother had her first kid at twenty, and she had one every year after that until she was twenty-eight. But even more significant, I think, was the difference in the structure of our families. Sam's father was a successful businessman. My parents both struggled to raise seven kids on mediocre research salaries. My mother always had to work. As far as I know, Zoe never worked while raising her three children. I was a very quiet kid who didn't even bother to fight for attention. I kept to myself. Sam was the oldest boy and his parents, his mother especially, adored him and still tell stories of how he behaved at three and four years old.

"I genuinely like my mother-in-law, but I don't feel very close to her. She is older than my own mother, more the age of a grandmother. I was very close to one of my grandmothers, who passed away a few years ago. So I don't have trouble relating to Zoe's age. I've always felt that she wants a close relationship with me. But she wanted that from the very start, which overwhelmed me. I take a while to develop friendships and trusting relationships, so I wasn't ready to embrace her or her family immediately. Since the early days of my marriage, I've been wary of opening up too much with her, as she is very close with all of her children and repeats 'family news' at will. Her kids even joke about 'the Mommy Net,' knowing that if they tell her something, their siblings will hear about it."

Relearning Family Skills

When new relationships are radically different from the kinds you are accustomed to, you must develop a whole new set of skills. The impulse is to draw upon your familiar repertoire, the way that Estelle calls upon her memories of her beloved grandmother. But just as parents recognize that their relationship with one child can be vastly different from their relationship with another child, every relationship needs individual attention. The more foreign it is, the more the work that needs to be done.

Estelle knows how to be with her mother, but how about her mother-in-law? She is still learning to pay attention to the specifics of this relationship. But she also feels that her mother-in-law doesn't value Estelle's great efforts to bring Sam closer to his family. "I think she would agree that we have a good, if not overly loving, relationship. But, now that I think about it, my brother-in-law, Sam's brother, once told me that his parents think I don't like them. I was hurt because I go out of my way for them in small ways. I pick up prescriptions, help with household chores, make sure Sam checks on them. . . ."

In addition, although Estelle didn't rank this high on her list of issues, she did note that coming in to her in-laws' family as Sam's second wife has affected her relationship with her mother-in-law. Sam's first wife was never considered part of the family, and Estelle felt that she had to surmount some barriers to be accepted. "This doesn't exemplify our relationship, but it did give us a rocky start. Once, my in-laws' neighbors were having a potluck holiday gathering. These neighbors have known each other forever, and they've known my husband since he was a kid. When Sam and I walked in, his mother greeted us with a warm and friendly 'Oh, here's Sam . . . and Felicia.' Sam's ex-wife's name is Felicia. It was one of those moments when the whole room gets quiet, and every person heard it. I smiled and said, 'Uh, it's Estelle' and my poor mother-in-law said, 'Of course it is. I know your name. That's what I meant to say.' I know that killed her and I tried to make light of it. But we were all thrown for a loop a bit."

Nadja, who has been married for seventeen years, has made it a policy to focus on the positive, not the negative. She believes it is more useful to be mindful of what is right in a relationship instead of what is wrong. She noted, "My upbringing and childhood were extremely different from my husband's. My husband comes from a home where the extended family was close. They were not perfect, but they were close and friendly. They helped each other and did things together. My family was not like that. Without going into detail, we were not close and we did not spend lots of time with family members. There was always a kind of tension in my family that clearly was absent in my husband's family.

"This has caused some difficulties in my marriage because I do not believe in forgiving and putting up with a lot of nonsense just because the person is a family member. This has caused some stress, particularly with my mother-in-law, because she feels that family is the most important thing in the world, and no matter what a person does, he or she is still family and should not be criticized. Usually, I just keep things to myself because most of his family members are really nice people, and I get along with all of them."

The Kinkeepers

Most people are partial to what they already know. It is always simpler to repeat patterns instead of modifying or creating new ones. We observed that many women want their family norms to supplant those of their spouses.

Sometimes this is the sanest choice, but sometimes it's just a reflex. Because women are most often the "kinkeepers," that is, those who preserve and continue traditions within a family, this role can cause stress when their traditions collide with those of their in-laws.

The role of kinkeeper can also cause problems with a spouse who brings a different set of traditions to the marriage. Is a daughter-in-law more likely to be comfortable in her marriage if her spouse adopts her family's customs and traditions and rejects his own? Different daughters-in-law have different answers to that question.

Ellen believed that her relationship with her mother-in law was a good one. She remembers that after she and Philip were engaged, she was welcomed with open arms. "They were thrilled," she said, "They couldn't believe their luck. I was college-educated, and headed for a teaching career. I wasn't pregnant and I was Jewish. They couldn't have asked for more."

But Ellen was brought up in a very affectionate and sharing family. She found the customs of her new in-laws odd and uncomfortable. For example, her mother-in-law received an allowance from her husband to run the household, whereas in Ellen's family, her parents had a joint bank account. Eventually, Ellen and her husband created their own family that reflected her family values much more than her husband's. What Ellen saw as a vastly different value system between her family and her husband's family made her interactions with her in-laws increasingly uncomfortable. She began to resent their intrusion into her life. "My parents worked together, shopped together, had one bank account, entertained often, always had pets, and raised flowers, birds, and tropical fish in addition to their kids. My husband never had a pet of any kind. His father spent a lot of time at the racetrack and, even though he was an attorney, he never provided much financial security for his family." Such behavior was shocking to Ellen. She found it very distressing and descrives her own parents as hard at work from "dawn until midnight." Their highest priorities were providing for their family and making sure their children's needs were met before their own.

Ellen explained, "They were totally bonded as a unit, and shared everything without question. Although my husband never felt deprived and often talks of the wonderful vacations his family had in Miami during the winter holidays, they were taking those vacations on next month's rent money. It is a testament to my husband's kindness and his love for his parents to view this as romantic instead of irresponsible," noted Ellen. "I, on the other hand, had parents who worked long hours. After years of working as milliners, my parents, finally, through investments and entrepreneurial drive, found success in the manufacturing industry. Financial security was important to them and they achieved this goal."

Early in their marriage, Philip worked for Ellen's parents, helping out in the new business. She believes that it was this close contact with her parents that had a major impact on Philip's value system and the way he grew as a marriage partner and father. Ellen said, "The good thing is that my husband became more like my family than his own. He is one of the most generous, devoted, attentive fathers and husbands that I have ever known. Our own family dynamics reflect my upbringing much more than his."

Nancy's husband, too, grew very close to his wife's parents and Nancy also said that her husband became more a part of her family than her becoming a part of his. Her mother-in-law is more like an absentee family member. Nancy commented that her mother-in-law does not "exercise her role as a grandmother" and prefers less involvement. "We all seem to talk and laugh and have fun and enjoy our time together, but my mother-in-law usually tells us she is too busy to visit: 'I have to clean my house; it's such a mess,' or 'I need to change my curtains,' and so on. She will not drop whatever she is doing to be with us at events. She is often too busy or feeling too ill to attend."

Men Without Sisters

We found that married men who have no sisters tend to have mothers who fit into two categories. Their mothers either want to or do consider their daughters-in-law to be like a daughter to them, or they find themselves fumbling through the new relationship. In Arnstein's study (1985), her interviews with specialists in the field pointed to the trend that women *without* daughters of their own tend to have a harder time in the role of mother-in-law.

Whether such women are more eager to embrace their "new daughter" as one of their own or are more awkward at integrating and adapting to the presence of another woman in the family circle, they may put undue pressure on their daughters-in-law. On the other hand, when the dynamics between the two women do work, a very special bond can develop between a mother-in-law and the daughter she never had, free of any jealousy or awkwardness that might be present if the mother-in law had her own daughter.

"I think one of the most important details about our dynamic is that my mother-in-law was never entirely satisfied being the only woman in the family," said Judith. "When my husband and I go to dinner at her house, nobody seems to listen to her, not my husband's father and not my husband either. She'll say, 'Something interesting happened at work today,' and my father-in-law will interrupt and say something like, 'Did you happen to get the windshield wipers looked at?' Now that she's got a 'daughter' around, the dynamic is slightly different. I have a woman's listening skills, so now she gets the follow-up questions that didn't come before. Now, she has someone to go shoe shopping with and to look through clothes catalogs with."

Judith finds the role of "instant daughter" difficult at times, but in her two years of marriage, she has noticed a change in her own attitude. Realizing that her mother-in-law is just as new at being around a daughter figure as she is at being a daughter-in-law, made a difference. She sees a compassionate relationship progressing with her mother-in-law. "I've learned a little bit more about her at each stage. Not all of it is good, but understanding her makes everything easier.

"I found her overbearing during the wedding planning. I was often frustrated with her and I know that she was frustrated with me. She would have loved to have shopped for the wedding dress with me, but I just couldn't bring myself around to include her. I know that, in some ways, I am the daughter she never had, and this was her chance to do that kind of mother-daughter thing. I felt bad, but I had to do what was right for me. We've settled down a lot since then, and we are a lot more on an even keel now."

No one is perfect, and Nel is very aware of that. Adoring her mother-in-law doesn't mean that everything is perfect every day or even that she agrees with everything her mother-in-law does. "The one fault I find with my mother-in-law is that she didn't encourage independence in her children. She was so capable and she did everything for them." This has taught Nel to facilitate her own children's independence. She feels she has learned valuable lessons from her mother-in-law; especially what to emulate and what to avoid. She and her mother-in-law enjoy a comfortable, compatible relationship that satisfies both women. Nel knows that she has a special place in her mother-in-law's heart. She knows she is the daughter her mother-in-law never had. She has felt like a "real" daughter to her mother-in-law since early in their relationship.

Arnstein (1985) also notes that mothers-in-law without daughters of their own are more likely to put unwarranted pressure on their daughters-in-law. However, most of the women we interviewed who married men without sisters found that they were accepted more readily than daughters-in-law who had to compete with "real" daughters.

"My husband had no sisters and my mother-in law treats me like I am the daughter she never had," said Jessica. "I think that mothers-in law who don't have their own daughters appreciate the chance to have that mother/daughter thing with daughters-in-law. We're appreciated more." Jan, whose husband also has no sisters, has found a special closeness with her mother-in-law, as well. "I wish we were both younger so we'd have more time to enjoy in the years ahead," she said.

Perhaps from the point of view of some mothers-in-law, having a daughter makes them more of an "expert," whereas, from the point of view of some daughters-in-law, being an "expert" is no guarantee of a good relationship.

Doris, who is an attorney and a writer of legal mysteries, also married a man who had no sisters. In spite of her many evident professional accomplishments, Doris' mother-in-law believed that Doris had "married up" because she came from a lower class than her husband's family. Doris' mother-in-law came from what she called "a very different social stratum." Clearly, the difficulties in this relationship were not due simply to the fact that Doris' mother-in-law had no experience with a daughter of her own. Doris, who considers her relationship with her mother-in-law both good and bad, has always felt that her mother-in-law sneered at her family of origin. When her mother-in-law invites Doris' family to visit her, Doris is expected to serve the food, clean, and attend to the needs of the household. Often, when Doris visits without her husband, she eats in the kitchen with the children while her mother-in-law and father-in-law dine in the dining room. "It was so awkward. I really didn't know how to approach this with my husband," she said.

Still, her mother-in-law was there for Doris during a very difficult pregnancy and she has tried to be supportive in other ways. Doris, whose relationship with her mother-in-law was problematic from the start, makes it clear that even in this difficult scenario, there are good things to be noted. "My mother-in-law truly doesn't understand what it means to display warmth. This does not mean she is a bad person. She was awkward as a mother and she certainly has a hard time relating to me as a daughter. I think the reality of my children has forced her to show her worst side to me. She must control me and her grandchildren as much as humanly possible. And even though this sounds awful, and sometimes is awful, her heart is in the right place. I do not doubt that she loves my children, and I want them to participate in that affection. My mother-in-law would raise them, if necessary. She would give them anything. They know they are treasured by this grandmother, even though her criticisms are hard to take."

Joy has the feeling that her mother-in-law is glad that she never had daughters, although her reasons are not rooted in a dislike of women. "Once my mother-in-law told me she was glad she never had a girl. She has four sons. We were shopping together, for clothes for me at the time. She likes to take me out, her treat, but she gets annoyed when I am too honest. I think she was aggravated because I was being more honest than usual about my likes and dislikes. When we got home, I called and told her she had hurt my feelings. She apologized. Recently, I unfortunately told her that if she'd had a girl, either her daughter would have killed her or vice versa. I haven't apologized yet."

Just Call Me "Mom"

What's in a name? Perhaps more than we think. A mother-in-law who wants her daughter-in-law to call her "Mom" is making a different statement than a mother-in-law who insists that her daughter-in-law call her "Mrs _____." "Mom" may not always feel right. It may feel awkward to a daughter-in-law, especially a new daughter-in-law, to use such an intimate name. Judith remarked, "My mother-in-law encouraged me on many occasions to call her 'Mom.' She signs cards to me with 'Mom.' I call her by her first name, though. It feels phony to call her 'Mom,' and in some ways, disrespectful to my parents."

Estelle negotiated this dilemma to suit her own level of comfort. "I generally avoid calling her anything. When my husband and I first got engaged, she asked if I'd like to call her 'Mom.' It didn't feel right then, and I guess it still doesn't. One of her sons-in-law, who has been married to her daughter for twenty-five years, still calls her 'Mrs. Sanderson.' I have referred to her as Mom Sanderson. I think calling her Mrs. Sanderson would only further what they think of my distancing. Besides, I'm Mrs. Sanderson, too, right?"

Nevertheless, using "Mom" may also feel welcoming and may help to foster a greater sense of intimacy. June notes, "At first I found it quite strange, even destabilizing, to call my mother-in-law 'Mom.' I already had one. I giggled a lot when I was trying it on for size. I had expected to call her by her first name and was nonplussed when I was given the 'Mom' answer to my question of how she would like to be addressed. I asked for it so I guess I had to live with it. It has only been a short time, but I've gradually learned to really appreciate it. She is a magnanimous woman, ready and willing to give of herself. 'Mom' now feels like the essence of maternal caring and thoughtfulness. Calling her 'Mom' also quickened my attachment. The name has power in and of itself. It shaped my experience of her and response to her. In retrospect, I think I was partial to calling her by her first name because I wasn't ready to integrate her, and in fact the whole clan, as family. I learned a valuable lesson."

"I call my mother-in-law 'Mom,'" explains Rivkah, a kindergarten teacher from Baltimore, "but that doesn't mean I feel like she's my mother. In fact, our relationship can be trying. I had few expectations when we married. Of course, I wanted to like her and for her to like me. She was warm and welcoming and things were fine. It was nice since my own family is less demonstrative."

Cross-culturally, there are different norms. Among families, traditions may dictate different choices of address. Some family traditions may not be or seem not to be a good fit. It can be hard to know what is right and this certainly presents a challenge.

Is It Good for You?

Testimony to a good relationship should not be defined by the amount of bliss generated by it. "Good" does not mean "easy" and it certainly does not mean the absence of conflict. Maintaining healthy relationships requires several skills, including the ability to disagree successfully. Also, "good" doesn't mean that matters will always flow smoothly and life will be easy. Life, in general, is not smooth and easy, so we cannot expect even the best relationships to be perfect all the time.

It would be unfair to hold the mother-in-law/daughter-in-law relationship to a higher standard than is possible to achieve. This would lead only to disappointment and hinder any chance of achieving a good relationship, since anything short of perfection would be deemed failure. Yet staying connected to someone imperfect can be tremendously challenging. You may have to endure and surmount great disappointments, and the ability to hold on in spite of disappointments can be trying.

Some daughters-in-law may have wonderful relationships with their mothers-in-law from Day One. This does not mean that there won't be disagreements that need to be addressed further down the line. The more complex and intimate a relationship becomes, the more likely it is that those involved will face disagreements. Finding a way to make a relationship function successfully with someone who may not have been chosen as a friend, and with whom there is now an intimate connection, is hard work. Clearly, judging from the words of several daughters-in-law in this section, what one person defines as "good" may be unacceptable to another. For the most part, a defining characteristic of these "good relationships" is an experience of mutuality between the two women. A supportive involvement in some capacity takes place, whether in a time of crisis or by gestures of inclusion and support. The meaning of "good relationship" is challenged when there are inherent difficulties between the parties; yet the relationship is not "bad" because it is not perfect.

Can we say that we can have a good relationship with someone we don't like? Can we have a functional relationship with someone who is dysfunctional? We might say that we can have a good relationship with someone we don't like, provided there is something about that person we do like. If there is nothing at all likeable about someone, no amount of tact and courtesy will force a good relationship.

In addition to sharing experiences of mutuality, another defining feature of good relationships is the capacity to acknowledge each other's goals and to recognize the importance of compromise and self-assertion. The daughters-in-law who were most optimistic about their relationships felt they could communicate needs or wishes that their mothers-in-law might not share. These daughters-in-law also felt confident that their personal boundaries would be respected. Furthermore, these daughters-in-law accommodated to the differences as well and did not expect all adaptations to be unilateral.

Where Do You Go from Here?

1. **Pay attention to uniqueness.** We learn from diversity. Accept that people bring their individuality into relationships.

2. **Take credit for things that work.** Women tend to attribute successful relationships to "luck," and when relationships are bad, they feel "guilty" or internalize blame. Luck implies arbitrary success. It is not arbitrary when relationships work well. You are instrumental in what works, as well as in what does not.

3. **Value what needs to be valued.** Notice attributes. Try to be mindful of strengths as well as of weaknesses.

4. **When drawing lines, draw them gently.** If you find the presence of your mother-in-law uncomfortable, or you think that she demands too much of your time, be thoughtful about how you address this issue with her.

5. **Be sensitive to your own mother.** Keep in mind that if your relationship with your mother is already difficult, appearing to replace her may be very painful to her. Try not to judge your mother/daughter relationship against your new, possibly more positive, relationship with your mother-in-law.

6. **Don't become complacent.** Even a healthy plant needs to be watered. Flourishing relationships require attention and thoughtfulness.

Summary Questions

* *What do you call your mother-in-law? Why was this choice made? How do you feel about it?*

* *What was your first impression of your mother-in-law?*

* *Did your relationship change during different periods (pre-marriage, pre-kids, etc.)?*

* *If you answered "yes" to the question above, to what do you attribute this change?*

Part II: The Bad

But when she was bad ...

Chapter 4

Bad Meaning Bad

I could tell even on our first visit that she was very house-proud. She has a nice house, filled with nice things that she cleans regularly. I could also see that she has a very powerful, confident, decisive personality. She doesn't dither and she thinks that she knows best.

—Sharon

One time she told me my oldest son (age two) was afraid of me. . . . He wasn't and still isn't! She based her comment on the fact that when I called him to me, he ran to her instead.

—Sophia

"Bad," like "good," is a vague term because it can mean so many different things to so many people. However, it can also serve as a benchmark or guide and allows us to view very different types of "not good" situations from the perspective of the daughter-in-law. Some people say that when you know it's right, you can feel it; and when you have to question whether things are good or not, then you might have a real problem.

Usually, we have positive feelings when a relationship is working. We use words like "easy" or "comfortable" to describe those feelings, just as we use words like "difficult" or "uncomfortable" to describe relationships that just don't seem to work as we hope they would. In a relationship as tenuous and as potentially loaded as that between mother-in-law and daughter-in-law, "uncomfortable" and "difficult" are words that make frequent appearances in conversations with daughters-in-law.

Is It Really So Bad?

To consider a relationship bad, one has to experience a level of discomfort that feels insurmountable. An element of pessimism is attributed to a bad relationship. Otherwise, "good" might still be the generalization employed because the hope still exists that the perceived difficulty might be overcome. Often the difference between good and bad will be in the perception of the daughter-in-law and how she proceeds in dealing with the relationship.

As in Part I, Part II deals primarily with what each daughter-in-law considers a bad relationship to be. No attempt has been made to create a set of objective qualifications that would define or quantify a bad relationship with one's mother-in-law. And, as in Part I, it will soon become clear that what one daughter-in-law perceives as bad may very well be an ideal, dream scenario to another daughter-in-law.

In Apter's (1999) research on the mother-in-law/ daughter-in-law relationship, she quotes a daughter-in-law who became furiously angry at her visiting mother-in-law for cooking breakfasts for the family, sewing buttons on the grandchildren's clothes, and washing and ironing the whole family's laundry. This daughter-in-law felt that her mother-in-law was making a clear statement that she believed her daughter-in-law was failing at her duties as a mother and wife. Armed exclusively with these complaints, we found many daughters-in-law who would have gladly offered this mother-in-law their services as daughter-in-law. However, since none of these would-be volunteers is the woman's actual daughter-in-law, there may be something here that they are missing. Perhaps these chores were performed passive-aggressively, or other signals of disapproval were conveyed. Then again, perhaps this mother-in-law's acts were simply misunderstood. Apter states that the daughter-in-law's often heightened sensitivity toward her mother-in-law is similar to the reactions of an adolescent daughter to her mother. Often, at that stage, the mother can do nothing right and everything she does is offensive to her daughter.

Lucy Rose Fischer, in her 1983 study, observed that the intimacy between a mother and daughter allows for both poor behavior and the criticism and confrontation that result from that poor behavior. However, in most mother-in-law and daughter-in-law relationships, that kind of room for overt conflict does not exist. Certainly, the unconditional love generally found in the mother/daughter relationship does not, as a rule, exist in the mother-in-law/daughter-in-law relationship. Fisher also says that because of that intimacy the same action performed by the mother-in-law or the mother can be viewed in totally different ways; for example, cleaning the kitchen. The mother may be seen as nurturing and helpful and the mother-in-law may be seen as intrusive or invasive. That perception of intrusion can lead to resentment and the gap between mother-in-law and daughter-in-law may grow even wider.

Sharon reluctantly classified her relationship with her mother-in-law as "bad," noting that it is "a low-grade bad." Because of her job as an administrator for a psychiatric practice for the past seven years, she has come into contact with many other women having difficulties in their family relationships. She has seen how differences in lifestyle and family life can create problems with in-law relationships. Considering her own case, Sharon feels that the differences between her and her mother-in-law are enormous. However, she also noted the positive aspects she sees in her mother-in-law's character.

"What I first noticed about her was that she had so much energy!" Sharon explained, "she's a small, slender woman who hardly ever stops moving. Once during our first visit she was running a carpet sweeper. Not a vacuum, but one of those little sweepers you push that picks up stuff with a rotating brush. It was like aerobic exercise, she practically *ran* around the room with it. I could tell even on our first visit that she was very house-proud. She has a nice house, filled with nice things that she cleans regularly. I was right to suspect that she would have problems with my house keeping. She doesn't dither and she thinks that she knows best."

But We Share So Much

A relationship can often have a promising beginning and then run into trouble. There are many factors that can contribute to a relationship's deterioration. Even when a mother-in-law and daughter-in-law have a great deal in common, there is the potential for serious conflict. Typically, finding common ground through upbringing, religion, or life choices can aid in creating harmony and, conversely, the lack of common experience can stimulate disharmony.

When a daughter-in-law brings to her marriage traditions that conflict with those of her mother-in-law's (and thus her husband's) upbringing, the tension may be great. These difficulties may intensify with the addition of children. Although the advent of children often reduces the amount of stress between mother and daughter, as a rule, children generally increase the stress between the mother-in-law and daughter-in-law (Arnstein 1985; Fischer 1983).

For example, the mother-in-law may view spanking as an acceptable form of discipline while the daughter-in-law finds it wholly unacceptable, or vice versa. The mother-in-law may see particular actions of the daughter-in-law as detrimental to her grandchildren's growth and development, but if she expresses herself too candidly to her daughter-in-law, she risks rejection and greater distance. Such distancing may threaten not only her relationship with her daughter-in-law, but her relationship with her grandchildren and, ultimately, her son. If the mother-in-law continues to convey negative judgments and does not honor her daughter-in-law's parenting choices, there is a high probability that this may endanger and possibly erode the family ties.

Of course, not every issue presents such a danger and being open to the benign suggestions of a more experienced woman can be helpful. New ideas can be enriching; however, the highly charged nature of this relationship can be perilous, as the wish for acceptance from the mother-in-law may be intense.

Generally, a daughter-in-law's, parenting practices reflect her own upbringing. Whether her choices are the same as her parents' choices were, or in opposition (i.e., she may have been spanked but she does not believe in corporal punishment), she is familiar with her parents' ways and most likely feels more at ease challenging her parents' opinions than challenging her in-laws' views.

Sophia is a social worker. She reflected, "Things were okay before the marriage, and since we are both Italian Catholics, I thought things would work out. But we think so differently. After the children came, things became worse and worse. One time she told me my oldest son (age two) was afraid of me.... He wasn't and still isn't! She based her comment on the fact that when I called him to me, he ran to her instead." Comments like these put Sophia on edge and cause her to resent the mere presence of her mother-in-law in her home. She cannot ignore such hurtful remarks and they make her nervous and defensive.

When Things Go Wrong

Jess had a good relationship with her mother-in-law for many years. She said, "Through the first nineteen years of my marriage, my relationship with my mother-in-law was, typically, harmonious." It was only when Jess and her husband began their own family that things became difficult. Having children significantly changed her relationship with her mother-in-law for the worse.

Jess said, "Since I had kids, my relationship with her has gone through some really difficult periods. The most difficult times coincided with those times we were unable to adapt our schedules to hers. Jess was quick to remark that her mother-in-law's inflexibility was not all-encompassing. Nevertheless, it was Jess who was always expected to make the majority of accommodations.

"As our children got older, and my husband's work demands became extremely high, typically, the only time we had together as a family was late Saturday afternoons and Sundays. My mother-in-law never once acknowledged how little time we had together and she always expected us to be at her beck and call."

Sharon, on the other hand, never felt that things were ever good with her mother-in-law and only fell apart later. Before marriage, however, she did have hopes for a positive relationship. "Before we married I had some romantic notions about learning to be her friend," she lamented. "She would teach me to cook my husband's favorite foods and tell me stories about him when he was a little boy. I thought she'd eventually realize what a good person I was and be very loving and kind toward me. But I am not blind to the way she sees me. I know that I am not the kind of person she would have chosen for her son. She thinks I am overly emotional, difficult, defensive, prickly, and impossible to understand. I know for sure that she thinks I'm a total slob."

Sharon described a critical event that marked the painful passage in her relationship with her mother-in-law. "About five days before our wedding, we were at the mall, doing some shopping with his whole family and my mother. I was wearing a loose jumper type of dress and his mother told me she liked it. That was good . . . for a minute I felt pretty happy.

"Then she followed her remark up by saying that I should always wear dresses and not pants (which I mostly live in) because I have a big butt. Whoa! Not that it's not true, I am overweight and I carry a lot of my weight in my behind and thighs, but that's not something I needed to hear at that time (or ever). I cried lots and lots of tears and I was so upset. The rest of the week I could barely enjoy my mom's cooking because I felt like my future mother-in-law was watching every bite I ate, and I was feeling very fat and unlovely at a time when I should have been happy. When my husband found out what happened, he was very supportive and told his mother that she had hurt my feelings. She was taken aback . . . after all she had just been telling me the truth and she had thought it was just helpful advice. She could not imagine why I was so sensitive."

Once bitten, twice shy, Sharon now feels stuck in a hypervigilant groove, expecting a slight from her mother-in-law at every turn. This tension further stifles the possibility of things ever going well. When a relationship becomes difficult, it can follow a downward spiral as matters take on a negative slant. Negative expectations can become self-fulfilling prophecies. Sharon is aware of this dilemma. "I wish I could stop caring so much about what she thinks of me," she confessed. "I know I am defensive, because I keep expecting her to say something about my weight, or how I dress, or my personal habits, or my housekeeping. If I could change one thing about our relationship, it would be that she could learn to see past all that stuff to the things my husband sees in me ... that I'm funny and smart, that I have a kind heart, and that I love her son very much."

Summary Questions

* *If you had three words to describe your mother-in-law, what would they be?*

* *If you had three words to describe your mother, what would they be?*

* *What do you consider the best thing about your relationship with your mother-in-law?*

* *What do you consider the worst?*

Chapter 5

The Space Between

We are both extremely strong personalities, but we have very different styles. We irritate each other. Sometimes she hurts my feelings so badly I really feel that I hate her.

—Sharon

In my heart of hearts I know it just kills her that her children are not being raised by a blue blood. She is doing everything in her power to make sure I raise them "right." I often feel that, to his family, my motherhood is a rent-a-womb proposition. They have proprietary rights in my children.

—Doris

After we were married, at least we were allowed to sleep in the same room on visits. When my daughter was born, we had more to talk about. Our child became the common point of interest. The baby made our time together easier.

—Hope

Often, there are such differences in social, cultural, and generational ideals that there seems to be no common ground on which to stand. Daughters-in-law and mothers-in-law may feel that they will never be able to have any kind of a successful relationship because of these disparities. When such differences are not respected, or come under attack, both parties may feel greatly hurt. Misreading a mother-in-law's actions is easy when the motives behind them seem foreign. When an awkward situation is ignored, resentment can grow. In this way, the negative can become the norm and the whole relationship can begin to worsen. The chasm will widen, making it more uncomfortable for everyone.

The Continental Divide and Other Chasms

Distance can be physical or symbolic but both constitute separation. A physical separation caused by two people living on separate continents presents obvious challenges. The barriers to the relationship may include language, lifestyle, customs, and cultural history. For example, Sharon's mother-in-law lives in Germany and many of Sharon's concerns reflect this distance.

"The truth is that we usually see my husband's mother only once a year," Sharon said. "The problem is that her visit may last for as long as two to three weeks. A couple of times, it's been twice a year and each visit was two to three weeks long! We rarely speak on the phone. We can communicate face-to-face, but it's difficult to overcome my bad German on the phone."

Sharon's distance from her mother-in-law is not just physical. "Although we are not outright hostile to one another, there is definitely tension between us," she said. "We are both extremely strong personalities, but we have very different styles. We irritate each other. Sometimes she hurts my feelings so badly I really feel that I hate her. I think she's too hung up on how she looks to the rest of the world. The only thing we have in common is my husband, her son.

"Another example of the tension," Sharon added, "is when we visit my in-laws; we stay upstairs, in my husband's old bedroom and office. Basically, we have a suite of three rooms and a bathroom. Now, I am, ordinarily, a messy type of person. Not dirty, you understand, just messy. I leave shoes strewn around the floor and I am perfectly happy to stack clean laundry on the couch for a couple of days before putting it away. I know that my mother-in-law is a *very* tidy, put-things-away-immediately type of person, so I always try to be neat in her house. I take my shoes off at the door and carry them to our room, I try not to leave things thrown down any which way. I hang clothes in the closet, I don't leave my toiletries out in the bathroom. But she still comes into our room to clean up, organizes our clothes, remakes the bed, puts things away. Argh. It drives me crazy. I know we are guests in her home, but can't she at least let us have *one* room that is *ours* while we are there?

"Also, our families are so different. My father is a college professor. My mother went to law school at night, got her law degree, and supported my dad while he got his Ph.D. Then she had me and my twin sister and stayed home to take care of us. We weren't rich, but we weren't poor either. My husband's parents both quit school to start working when they were teenagers, to help out their families. Life in Germany was hard after the war. They married young and had my husband almost immediately. I think their lean years were over about the time my husband started high school, and now they are fairly well off.

"I finally realized that my mother-in-law and I *had* to be in each other's lives. So now, when I see her, I try *very hard* to be pleasant. Not that she doesn't still drive me crazy, but I try harder to hold on to my temper, so as not to cause my husband pain. I also had a long talk with one of my husband's friends in Germany and she said something that made me willing to try even harder to be kind and less ready to take offense with my mother-in-law's habits. The friend said that, at our wedding, she could see my mother-in-law felt sad that her son was marrying and choosing to live so far from home. He is her only child and he lives so far away that she'll probably see him only once a year for the rest of her life. For someone who lives within a ten-minute walk of the rest of her family, I can see how that's difficult. That insight made me more sympathetic to her than I had ever felt before," Sharon notes empathetically.

Cultural differences also play a role in Sophia's difficult relationship with her mother-in-law. They are both Italian, but were brought up very differently. Different child-rearing practices do not inherently cause conflict, just as similar practices do not inherently create harmony. However, clashing lifestyles may require negotiation and accommodations that the familiarity of similar upbringings or lifestyle choices may not. Fundamental differences do make some degree of accommodation and compromise necessary. Sophia was brought up in a modern Italian family in the United States. Her mother-in-law was from "the old country" with intensely prominent "old country" ways. Sophia wanted more sharing and closeness with her mother-in-law, but she came to realize that this was not possible because, for her mother-in-law, the discussion of certain intimate matters is unacceptable.

Getting Colder

Dana, too, has always felt alienated from her mother-in-law. She always believed that the gap between them was due to their religious differences. She was raised as an Episcopalian in a freer, more open household than her husband was. Her mother-in-law is a Jehovah's Witness, which Dana sees as a highly restrictive theology. Dana describes their relationship as, "Warm because I love her as my husband's mother. Distant because she did not attend my first daughter's baptism because she said I made her feel 'uncomfortable.' To this day I believe it was a religious issue. We have never had a close relationship since that occasion." Dana also said that she and her husband were raised in very different kinds of home environments. "My husband was very much secluded from friends. His family's religion did not permit them to do anything on Saturdays. And, he was sent away to live at his high school, which was religion-related."

In the early stages of their relationship Dana found her mother-in-law energetic and fun to be with. She had hopes her mother-in-law would like her and that the relationship would work, despite their differences. But matters began to deteriorate when Dana had children. "Once the kids were born our relationship changed. I felt that she judged me harshly because I was not the same religion and didn't view life in the same way that she did."

Dana, like Sophia, has not achieved an open discourse with her husband in regard to his mother. She has never felt that she could speak to her husband about his mother. She said, "I try to keep my mouth shut. Whatever my husband wants I try and go along with." Although she seems to have resigned herself to this situation, and sees no alternative, this will not prove to be a constructive strategy for improving the situation.

The sources for familial or cultural differences are rooted in tradition. These disparate traditions can be a great cause of discomfort. A daughter-in-law need not come from a foreign country to encounter extremely different customs in her husband's family. But a healthy marriage blends two people and their cultures into one. Rather than trying to exclusively replicate the other spouse's traditions (unless this is by mutual choice), the couple can learn to choose elements from both upbringings to enrich their new family.

Trying to impose traditions can have an adverse effect. When a mother-in-law is too controlling, it undermines the successful development of autonomy and identity of the couple *as a couple*. If a mother learns to vacate the role of First Lady gracefully, allowing her daughter-in-law to step in to the role, there is an opportunity for a smooth transition and a welcoming of new ideas.

Mrs. Mother-In-Law

Schisms can be created by patterns of behavior that send negative signals. What is comfortable and familiar to one person may be off-putting or alien to another. A daughter-in-law may feel that her mother-in-law is rejecting when she perceives her mother-in-law's message as negative, whether it is intentional or not. The daughter-in-law may pull back, and the gap may grow wider.

For example, Doris, who we first met in Chapter 3, was told at the beginning of her marriage that she was to address her mother-in-law as "Mrs." As far as Doris was concerned, this chilled the temperature of the entire relationship, leaving Doris at a very long arm's length. The rejection that Doris experienced with her mother-in-law felt like her mother-in-law was reinforcing the sentiment that Doris was not the woman her son should marry.

Doris' in-laws are from very old New England families. Their genealogies go back two hundred years. Doris' mother-in-law had not been a very doting mother. She was very involved in meeting social obligations and never felt that it was her role to cater to her children. Nevertheless, she loves her sons very much, and saw to it that they were properly brought up and went to the proper schools.

Doris is from a farming family in Indiana. Her parents were first-generation children of Ukrainian immigrants, and her father left the family when she was twelve. "For a while, effectively, we were homeless, but for the charity of the Lutheran Church. Once we lived in a trailer on one church member's property. My husband's family have never moved from the house they built down the hill from his paternal grandfather's house. They have owned that land since the mid-1700s. My husband moved away for the first time when he left home for college.

"My mother-in-law threw me a wedding," explained Doris. "My husband and I had planned to elope in secret, but he told his mother, and she insisted on us having a church wedding. I was not opposed to a church wedding but I had no time and no money and no dowry to pull one together. She insisted on doing it. I was grateful to her, and she was pleased with my gratefulness. I also let her do anything she wanted. She was paying for it, planning it, and hosting a reception at her house. I could hardly complain. Truthfully, I was glad she did this, and I am still glad we had that wedding. *But,* looking back, it set a precedent for our future relationship: Whatever she wants, she gets. I do not argue. I do what she asks."

Another precedent set by Doris' mother-in-law was the form of address that Doris was instructed to use. Doris said, "She made it clear to me that she had addressed her mother-in-law as 'Mrs. La Butte' and I was to do the same. But I would like a more balanced, adult relationship. Mrs. La Butte is not a warm and fuzzy handle. Sometimes, I wish we were more like friends, but I do not need her friendship. I have many caring friends. And she is not equipped to warm up to me in that way. Her generation, her place in the world, were more formal. She likes that formality and the clear expectations of proper behavior. She and I are very different from one another. It would be nice to feel she accepted me as I am, but I think I will always be a work-in-progress for her."

Helen, on the other hand, doesn't really care whether calling her mother-in-law "Mrs." is a tradition or not. She refuses to participate in it. "I don't call her anything. I told her that I already had a mother, and I refused to call her Mrs. Lindbergh." Helen and Doris have much in common: both women, when adolescents, experienced parental divorce; both of their husbands' parents were married more than fifty years; both of their husbands have only brothers as siblings; both have mothers-in-law who created distance between themselves and their daughters-in-law; and both found their difficulties increased with the arrival of their children.

But Helen and Doris also reacted in very different ways to their similar circumstances. Helen had expected to be taken into the family by her mother-in-law. She had hoped for a closeness which, to her great disappointment, she did not find. "I expected to be treated with the same respect as I treated her. I expected to love her because she is my husband's mother."

For Doris, it was different. "I had no real expectations. If anything, I expected I would rarely see her and that our lives would be fairly independent from one another. I did not plan on having children when I married. We thought we would have our professional lives and that would be more than enough. But my biological clock started ticking and, lo and behold, we had two children."

Doris is much more passive in her relationship with her mother-in-law than Helen, and she did not have the energy or temperament to challenge her husband's mother. Acquiescence was much more her style than confrontation. But that doesn't mean it makes her feel good. She said, "I think she finds me usually compliant and eager to please. She has the upper hand and likes it that way. She has given little, if any, thought to how her actions affect my feelings or those of my children. She is oblivious to her effect on anyone. But I would like to like her more."

Helen's mother-in-law is also very controlling. She said, "After I had kids, our relationship got worse. My mother-in-law belittled just about everything I did. Then my husband was laid off, and he took two classes at the community college. My mother-in-law baby-sat Rebecca at her house until I came home from work. I was breast-feeding, and she didn't approve of the practice. She insisted on having a bottle the two hours that Rebecca was there. I said she didn't need a bottle. I said I would feed her when I got home at 5:30. She got a bottle from her neighbor. I don't know what she put in it. I found out about it about five years later."

Doris' mother-in-law didn't breast-feed her children. She, too, did not embrace the practice, but she did make a special nursing blouse for Doris. Also, Doris had a very difficult pregnancy with her first son. She stayed at her mother-in-law's home and felt that she was in good hands. "Good controlling hands," but good hands nonetheless.

Helen feels that her mother-in-law's judgments are overbearing and unfounded. She thinks they express a very different set of values than her own. "After we had our first child, I was told I didn't dress my daughter in the right clothes, which would have been little fancy dresses. In her eyes, a good mother always dressed her children in fancy clothes. The important things about raising a child—nurturance, love, manners, values . . . none of that counts in her eyes.

"My husband just tunes her out. I had never experienced such nagging before I met her! I wanted her to like me, so I dealt with her. After my last child, I realized dealing with her was my husband's job. Since I survived breast cancer, though, we have a more tolerable relationship. She doesn't make nasty comments to me anymore."

Although Doris' has felt the impact of classism from her mother-in-law, she has found strength in her own history and future. She said, "Fortunately, although I am a great granddaughter of immigrants, I set my sights high educationally and, to some extent, socially. I want my children to be confident and to feel at ease with anyone, queen or peasant. As unlikely as it may seem, my goals for my children are not much different than my mother-in-law's goals for them. Nonetheless, she doesn't completely trust me with the job."

Doris is generous, however, and she finds some of her mother-in-law's behavior forgivable. She said, "She has strong opinions about people's appearances. She is particularly harsh in her judgments about my children's hair, clothing, manners, and so forth. She is equally harsh about my appearance. A common scene over the years has been for us to arrive at her house, run combs through our hair while we are in the car, and still be greeted with, 'Comb your hair.' This often leads to her insistence that, at least the children (and often I am included), be whisked off directly to her hairdresser."

Like Helen's husband, Doris' husband was unaware of his mother's behavior to his wife. His recent involvement has made a difference. "About a year ago," said Doris, "my mother-in-law included her son in her criticism. He told her absolutely 'no.' He would not go to her hairdresser. It was the first time he saw the pressure she has regularly put on me and the children in this department. That was when I began to believe that my husband could be my ally in this relationship with his mother."

For both Helen and Doris, an important change in their family dynamics took place when their husbands became active participants in their family interactions with their mothers. Doris explained, "Up until the last year or two, my mother-in-law mostly communicated with me, not with her son. He and his brother stopped listening to what she had to say long ago. This made me the keeper of the family calendar and the one who had to deal with her strong opinions and controlling behavior. It caused great difficulty for me. My personality is not as strong as hers. I tend to yield to a stronger force, but it was taking a toll, and after ten years or so, I surrendered."

For Doris, being passive in the face of her mother-in-law's controlling behavior caused her little difficulty. But she saw that her children were hurt by her mother-in-law's behavior. That was the impetus for her to change. "I finally began to argue with her, for the sake of my children. Fortunately, my husband is better able to stand up to her than I am. These days I direct most communications to him and he deals with her most of the time."

Still, for Doris, there will always be some discomfort with her mother-in-law. "In my heart of hearts I know it just kills her that her children are not being raised by a blue blood. She is doing everything in her power to make sure I raise them 'right.' I often feel that, to his family, my motherhood is a rent-a-womb proposition. They have proprietary rights in my children. When my son looked like my brother, they said he looked like no one. They are so relieved that he is beginning to favor his great-uncle, my mother-in-law's brother."

His Mother's Child

Although it can be hard for a wife when her mother-in-law is intrusive, often, it is her husband who feels the intrusion most keenly. A man's mother may have difficulty relinquishing the role she played for the entirety of her son's life. If she was a doting mother, her married son may now find such doting overbearing. In addition, he may be trying to separate and individuate from his family of origin at the same time that his wife may be trying to form a connection with her in-laws. These opposing efforts may create strain for the couple.

Nadja believes that it is her own issues that make matters uneasy at times. She does not think her mother-in-law is guilty of being invasive. "She does not throw her weight around," Nadja explained. "Things have remained very constant over the last seventeen years. She and I still get along very well, but there are times when I think my husband placates her and doesn't 'side' with me. It is not a huge issue because she is so good to both of us."

In this regard, Estelle noted, "Sam can be somewhat passive; he doesn't let much bother him. But he's not very proactive either. He loves his mother quite a lot, so he doesn't let her know when she's acting overbearing. He also doesn't call her regularly without my encouragement. So, though I suspect she wishes that she and I were closer, she probably doesn't realize that I am largely responsible that Sam maintains *their* closeness."

When Judith talked about how matters were between her husband and his mother, she said: "The relationship between my husband and his mother is tense and is growing more and more so. He's trying to make an adult break and she is trying to hold on to him. For a while, I felt that she must blame me for his very overt desire for more space—away from her. He asked her not to call us as often—or at least to save up all of her questions for one phone call, and not to call me at home during the day. She called up later and asked, 'How often am I allowed to call?' Now, most of the time, she makes my husband's father do the dialing. It's obvious that she's behind the phone call because my father-in-law dials up and says, 'What did you think of the basketball game? Oh, and by the way, there's a pot of soup and a cantaloupe in the refrigerator here that you're welcome to.'"

Frequently, in addition to maintaining her own delicate balance with her mother-in-law, a daughter-in-law also finds herself negotiating her husband's relationship with his mother. Judith described the situation this way: "The hardest part is that my husband can be quite harsh with her in a way that makes me uncomfortable. I never threw tantrums with my parents when I was a teenager, I never did the whole 'I hate you,' slamming-the-door bit. My husband, on the other hand, is a real firecracker and he lets her know when she's overstepped her bounds. Recently, she tried to straighten his collar for him, and he took her hands off him in a very angry way. She went into a pout and the whole evening went downhill from there."

Hope, on the other hand, observed that the strain she feels with her husband in regard to his parents is that she has begun to see that he is much more like his parents than she had thought when she met him. "When we were younger, I didn't notice or maybe I didn't care that Steve was somewhat distant. I'm very expressive. Steve is like his mother. They are both emotionally reserved. I'm more passionate; he's more passive. After our daughter was born and with my business practically running itself, I began to feel alienated by his emotional absence. My parents were living in Ohio and I felt very alone. I certainly couldn't speak to my mother-in-law about anything and I felt that, in that same way, I couldn't speak to Steve. He is a dear man, but he feels somewhat removed to me. I see his mother in him much more than I did when we were courting."

Hope has a very intimate relationship with her own family. "We're close in a serious way," Hope said. "I mean, we fight and yell at each other, but we joke around and do a lot of laughing. As far as I can tell, my mother-in-law has no sense of humor whatsoever. Steve's folks are old-time Iowa farmers. They are also very religious. Before we were married, Steve and I had been living together for a year and we had to hide it from his folks. After we were married, at least we were allowed to sleep in the same room on visits. When my daughter was born, she became the common point of interest, and made our time together easier."

This is a good example of how hollow a civil, courteous, and polite relationship between a mother-in-law and daughter-in-law can be. "Good" relationships depend on much more than good manners. Many relationships that are challenging and difficult at the outset can achieve deeper and more satisfying outcomes. Without change and progress, any relationship becomes stagnant. Without substance, there is little with which to work.

Hope and Steve have been married for eight years and, unfortunately, little has changed in Hope's relationship with her husband's mother. "My interactions with my mother-in-law continue to be strained and superficial. There is no genuine *anything*. Also, Steve and his mother rarely communicate. They have almost no relationship whatsoever; however, when they do talk, it's at least polite. If you asked my mother-in-law to tell you one thing about me, one thing I liked or disliked, one thing that was interesting to me, I don't think you'd get a genuine answer. She truly doesn't know me in the least."

A Different Me

There are many reasons why a daughter-in-law, when she is with her mother-in-law, might behave differently than she would with her own family or friends. She may feel a desire to impress or please her mother-in-law and may thus obscure or disguise her true self. Or she may change over time during the course of her marriage. She may go through great personal changes that cause her connection with her mother-in-law to feel less fulfilling, and to be in need of change. When daughters-in-law discuss their mothers-in-law, the complaint, "She doesn't know me," is extremely common. It is also not uncommon to hear daughters-in-law say that, when their mothers-in-law are around, they can never act like themselves.

Sophia's discomfort around her mother-in-law causes her to behave in ways that, normally, she would not. For Sophia, her own unusual behavior intensifies the uncomfortable quality of their interactions. For example, Sophia said, "Normally, I think I have a warm, friendly tone of voice. But when I speak to her, my voice flattens, and all feeling drains out of it. There were many upsetting events over the course of my marriage that led to this state of affairs." Naturally, by behaving in such unnatural ways, Sophia estranges her mother-in-law even further, and Sophia feels even more strongly that her mother-in-law does not have a clue as to who she is.

Emma felt that "during the dark years" she found it very uncomfortable to behave naturally in her mother-in-law's presence. "I was always on guard for some gesture or word that would set us back even further. I felt she was just waiting for me to mess up." When Emma wasn't trying to watch her step, she was trying to step out of the way. And, she observed, her mother-in-law was doing the same thing. "I see now how we both were so guarded that neither of us ever allowed the other to see who we really were. I guess the question is how can you ever know someone, or let them know you, if everyone is acting like someone else?"

Perhaps there is good reason to feel guarded. It cannot be denied that some daughters-in-law are scrutinized and attacked by their mothers-in-law. The hope is that daughters-in-law can develop the confidence they need to relax some of their defensive façades. By acting more authentically they may begin to feel more understood. This will give their mothers-in-law a chance to see them "as they really are."

It took many years for Astrid's mother-in-law to acknowledge Astrid as the upstanding woman she is. Astrid was a homemaker who returned to school at age forty-two and received her doctorate in bioethics. She found early in her marriage that she was totally alienated by her mother-in-law, Kara. Astrid said, "When I first met Kara I was really intimidated. Her background, experience, and huge reputation in the community were all very different from mine. Although my husband, Sven, apparently was her favorite child, Kara was polite but very distant with me. It wasn't because I was taking away her son, but simply because she was not interested in me. She had a demanding medical practice, many professional friends (mostly men), and many social relationships. She had no room in her life for me."

Kara was very domineering. Astrid said, "I was given *no choice* about having Kara as my pediatrician. She would not have tolerated my having another doctor for her grandchildren. Also, Kara had no interest in 'pleasing' the mothers who were her clients. Parents were never given the opportunity to ask questions, or make suggestions, or second-guess the treatment. And if you failed to follow her directions, you were in for a nasty scolding. I was treated exactly like all her other patients. However, even with the best doctor in town for my sons, I would advise any other daughter-in-law to pass on having grandma as your pediatrician.

"When my son, Jens, was born, my relationship with my mother-in-law did not change. By that time, however, I was more sure of myself and I had a life of my own. In truth, I didn't miss having a relationship with her and knew that I had the best doctor in town even though she was the general and I had to salute.

"She had absolutely no interest in me until I entered graduate school . . . and even then she was not particularly interested in me until I received my doctorate and went to work. Clearly being her daughter-in-law, or wife to her son, or mother of her grandchildren gave me no status, but being a professional, I had credibility. Also, I know she was getting close to the end of her life and she realized that, other than for her small immediate family, she was alone. She had been widowed for nearly twenty years, and her practice had diminished. Although she was caring for third and fourth generation children, many parents did not want to use her, assuming that she would die before their children were teenagers.

"I believe she had a hard time learning how to be friends with me—as a woman. I don't think she had ever had a close female friend before. It was easy for me to respond to her overtures and to overlook her previous coldness. I was proud of myself and I enjoyed receiving her respect . . . never praise, though. We became good friends, and we talked about the personal things that women talk about, as well as our mutual interest in children's issues. She had lived through so many generations and changing parental styles. She brought a fascinating perspective to these issues. We shared books and stories. The last three years of her life she became very dependent on me. We had both changed. I have no doubt that the changes we both experienced as we grew older allowed us to grow closer."

Children and Family Dynamics

In general, having children changes all familial relationships. Once a daughter-in-law becomes a mother, a host of new responsibilities become hers. This is a major developmental passage that, along with the joy, necessarily invokes stress and havoc within the woman herself, and in many of her relationships. Often, these changes are a source of tension between mother-in-law and daughter-in-law.

Jess noticed the biggest change with her mother-in-law occurred when she had her third child. This is when the relationship became the most difficult it had ever been. Jess said, "During the last six years, several factors contributed to difficulties in my relationship with my mother-in-law. I had another child, both my in-laws retired, and my husband continued to believe it necessary to please his parents and meet their demands, even when it was not good for our immediate family."

The addition of a third child had a much more pronounced effect on Jess' family dynamics than she had ever expected it would. She said, "At forty years old, I had our third child. The gap between my oldest and youngest is thirteen years. Rather than the new child just slipping into a settled family life, as my other two children had, the addition of the new baby brought on a period of chaos.

"We had not understood or appreciated how a number of factors would impact on our lives, many in very significant ways. The first was my mother had died five years before the baby was born. She had provided a lot of hands-on help when my other two children arrived." The lack of this support had a great impact on Jess. "I had to meet the additional work and time demands of a new child with much less help. My mother-in-law was working full-time and did not take any time off to help me.

"The second thing was, we had not fully appreciated how the vast differences in the ages of our children would affect the demands on our time. I had always handled the children's schedules on my own. Trying to meet two children's school, athletic, scout, and religious commitments while bringing along a baby proved very challenging. Another problem was that our oldest child had just reached the age where he began to rebel against our parental authority. Eventually, we had to deal with a number of stressful events he was mixed up in. Then, my husband had just started a new law firm the year before the baby was born. He had to give most of his time and energy to this venture."

During these very stressful times, Jess found herself less and less comfortable with the social demands her mother-in-law was making. "There were times when she wanted us to come to visit, or when she would have liked to visit at our house. My husband likes to please his mother and he couldn't understand why it wasn't a good idea for his parents to visit. Naturally, dealing with that was stressful, too."

One of the first tasks facing a new couple is to create a new context of family that is separate from their in-laws. Many of the daughters-in-law in Part II have not successfully completed this developmental challenge. The struggle is to create a working blueprint that allows them to make the transition from their families of origin and those of their spouses to a separate one of their own.

Summary Questions

❋ *Is there something you would like to change about your relationship with your mother-in-law? How would you like to approach this change?*

❋ *How comfortable are you with the following dimensions regarding your relationship with your mother-in-law? On a scale from 1 (least comfortable) to 10 (most comfortable), how would you rate the following factors in your relationship?*

- *Communication* _____

- *Attention* _____

- *Respect* _____

- *Involvement* _____

- *Warmth* _____

❋ *Can you elaborate on your choices?*

❋ *If you had one wish for the relationship, what would it be?*

Chapter 6

Stand by Your Woman

I wish she would not be so overprotective of her son and understand that I also contribute to the outcome of our marriage and of the raising of our children.

—Sophia

What I think about the "dynamic" between my husband, his mother, and me is, well, here we have two strong, opinionated women, both used to getting their way most of the time, with nothing in common except one man. We both want to be "the most important" woman in his life. But if we ever really took our gloves off and started fighting, the only thing we'd accomplish would be to hurt that man; so, we just try to be civil to each other.

—Sharon

In her experience as a social worker, Sophia has spoken with many women about their difficulties at home and the problems that they faced with their spouses and their spouses' mothers. When she looks at her own life, she sees that her relationship with her husband continues to be strained by her issues with her mother-in-law. "Many of the arguments I have with my husband have been about the way his mother treats me," she said. "He is so close to his mother that I would never say anything 'negative' about her."

Her husband placed the entire burden of making an accommodation with his mother on Sophia's shoulders. Unable to discuss her mother-in-law problems with him, she felt unprotected. "He would tell me that because I was a 'trained professional' it was up to me to be the 'better' person in my dealings with her. Consequently, many of our arguments were not about her, but about my feeling unsupported by my husband."

By making Sophia the only one responsible for deciding the fate of the relationship with his mother, Sophia's husband removed himself from the role of partner. By making the subject of his mother's behavior completely off-limits for complaints, or even discussion, he removed the possibility for any genuine exchange regarding Sophia's struggle.

The Woman of the House

Historically, and in the majority of cultures around the world, women have not had the freedom that men had. Running the household and taking care of the children have been the traditional roles for women. Those responsibilities were often passed down from one generation to the next, often from mother-in-law to daughter-in-law. Little, if any, emphasis was placed on the quality of the relationship. How a woman felt was not given much weight nor was it ever considered particularly important, so long as she did her job, whether it was cleaning the house or looking lovely.

In modern culture, we are much more aware of happiness, the quality of communication, and candid interaction than our forebears. Sophia notes, "I wish my mother-in-law would realize that I contribute to the outcome of our marriage and of the raising of our children." By not giving Sophia any credit, or at least giving Sophia the impression that she doesn't give her any credit for raising the family, her mother-in-law invalidates Sophia's importance within her own family. This causes Sophia to feel profoundly devalued. Sophia lamented that her mother-in-law conveys the message that she, not Sophia, is the important maternal figure in the lives of Sophia's children and husband. In Sophia's eyes, her mother-in-law still considers herself "The Mama."

Joy said, "When my mother had a heart attack two years ago, I was trying to figure out how to help her handle her life. I am the one among my siblings who was most in a position to be 'in charge' of what to do for our mother. When sorting out my thoughts, at first, I was listening to my husband and mother-in-law's opinions. They advised me to put my mom's house on the market and look for a nursing home for her. I was nearly ready to do that. My mother's spirit seemed to be waning. But I consulted with one of my mom's best friends. All she said was, 'Joy, I think you should try it out and see how your mom manages at her own home,' and she offered to help me with the transition. Right then and there I made the decision, *without* consulting my husband—or my mother-in-law.

"I went home and told my husband what I was going to do, and he said, that if I did that, then he would 'withdraw his love and affection.' I told him to do what he had to do. I was deeply hurt and extraordinarily upset by his stance, but I went ahead with what I had decided to do. It was a very scary time for me. Weeks later, I told my husband that I thought he owed me an apology for threatening to withdraw his love and affection. He apologized.

"To this day my mother is living in her own home about an hour away from us in Upper Montclair. I have hired round-the-clock care for her. I take care of her bills and yard, and I visit her about once a week. Sometimes, I skip a week. The reason my husband originally objected to my choice was that he thought that, if I kept my mother at her own home, it would make more work for me and that would be more of a drain on our family life. What he never understood, and I'm still not sure he does understand, was that I would be much more stressed if I had put my mother into a nursing home, and she died sooner, than if I maximized the quality of her life and she lived longer. I didn't want her death on my conscience, and I have the skills to do what I'm doing.

"My mother-in-law disapproves strongly of the choices I made to allow my mother to go on living in her own home. This has been hard for me to handle, but I am as clear as I can be about the choices I made. I *am* angry that my mother-in-law doesn't really appreciate what I've done, although she does say she admires the way I 'juggle' everything. I am also resentful that she has the gall to think she knows better than I do what's best for *my* mother. Once I stopped running around making sure the sky wasn't falling in, I could see things more clearly. I keep telling her that she only has a window into our lives."

Helping Hands

Rivkah, whom you first met in chapter 3, said that the lack of helpful support from her mother-in-law when she visits Rivkah's house has created a good deal of irritation on Rivkah's part. "My mother-in-law is much less helpful than my mother," she noted. "She will not clear her place after a

meal or help around the house. She expects to be served and
waited upon. Even when I had the baby in my arms, or I was
changing diapers, she would not lift a finger to help. However, since it is my house, she may feel that she is stepping
on my toes, and I try to understand.

"My mother-in-law was very anxious before my daughter was born. I was hospitalized at thirty-four weeks with
preeclampsia and was pretty miserable. My mother-in-law
would call my room several times a day, sometimes twice in
an hour, ask me a million questions about the baby, and she
never once asked if it was a bad time to be calling, or if I'd
prefer not to talk. She'd do this night after night. I couldn't
handle it, so I insisted that my husband, Benjamin, talk to
her, and answer her questions.

"Benjamin protects his parents, but he is learning they
aren't perfect. I have to be very gentle if I want to give him
feedback about them, or make a request of them through
him. My mother can be very 'in your face,' but I never have
felt the same intrusiveness from her. It might be because
she's my own mom, but it is also the way people are. It's like
my mother-in-law has gone overboard with the concept that
I am the woman of my house. It's like she thinks she should-
n't have to lift a finger to do anything, unless she is specifi-
cally asked."

Power struggles abound in Sharon's relationship with
her mother-in-law. "When we bought our house," she
remembers, "my mother-in-law bought us a couch. She and
my father-in-law were here to help us fix the house up.
When we went to order the couch, she went straight to a
particular sofa and said it was the best one for us. Well, I sat
on every sofa in the store, because that is just the kind of
shopper I am. I *have* to try everything out, even if I eventually choose the first one. I came back and agreed with my
mother-in-law that the one she liked was a good size and
shape for our living room. Then I went to choose the

upholstery fabric. I looked and looked at fabrics, comparing them with a paint chip I brought from home. Meanwhile, my mother-in-law was muttering to my husband in the background. He finally came to me and told me that she wanted to know why I was looking for a different fabric; why didn't we just have the couch covered with the same fabric the store model was covered in?

"I tried to explain that I wanted a different look, but nothing I said convinced her. We finally ordered the couch in *my* fabric, but all the while she kept saying she thought I was making a bad mistake. It just ruined the whole experience for me. I was grateful she bought us a couch, but her attitude and the way she tried to control the decision took the joy out of the gift. My mother-in-law is not a bad person, but we are just so different, and there is so much prickliness in my feelings toward her, that almost any generous thing she does leaves me with some kind of negative feeling."

Although Sharon complained about her mother-in-law, we heard very little about her husband's input on the decisions. The absence of input from her husband suggests that the couple may be having difficulty functioning as partners. Time and time again Sharon has been annoyed or angered by her mother-in-law's vocal dominance and intrusive manner. At some point, she needs to recognize where the pitfalls are, and learn how to avoid them. She sets herself up by accepting gifts that come with a price; a price she doesn't want to pay. When you can see clearly what lies ahead by looking clearly at what came before, you may be able to sidestep obvious or anticipated landmines.

Sharon recognizes that she shares some responsibility for her predicament. She said, "What I think about the 'dynamic' between my husband, his mother, and me is, well, here we have two strong, opinionated women, both used to getting their way most of the time, with nothing in common except one man. We both want to be 'the most important' woman in his life. But if we ever really took our gloves off and started fighting, the only thing we'd accomplish would be to hurt that man; so, we just try to be civil to each other.

"My husband knows that I irritate his mother and she irritates me. I used to gripe to him about his mother a lot, but one day he said that every time I did that, I really hurt him. He said he loved me *and* he loved her, and it made him sad and upset when he had to listen to me run his mother down. That made me stop and think, and from that time on I have tried hard to bite my tongue and not complain to him about his mother. After all, she is his mother, and while she's not perfect, they love each other very much. It's interesting, too, since I quit griping about her to him, he's much quicker to speak up if she does something that annoys him. I guess that since he doesn't feel like he always has to defend her from my anger, he can say it when he is annoyed with her."

Balancing Act

Sharon's insight about her husband is an important one. All relationships generate an equilibrium—whether bad or good. Over time, individuals develop patterns in their particular roles to maintain that equilibrium. Sometimes the roles become rigid and fixed. One person may always ends up as the irresponsible one, the dependable one, the angry one, or the emotional one, and so forth. In other words, one person becomes the designated container or carrier of a certain behavior or set of emotions. This often leaves no room for the other person to also inhabit this space. When Sharon took a step back from her anger, her husband was able to relinquish his defensive posture and own up to some of his own angry feelings.

My Husband, Your Son

Tsong was brought up in the same country as her mother-in-law. While still a child, she and her parents escaped the horrors of war and fled to England. There she met and married her husband, who was also a refugee. Her family suffered greatly, but she and both of her parents survived. Her mother-in-law was not as fortunate. When she arrived in Dover as a refugee, she had lost her husband and had only her children left.

Tsong's parents were highly educated professionals. Tsong's mother-in-law was illiterate and her children were all she had. She lived for them. From the start, these differences prejudiced the relationship between Tsong and her mother-in-law. With time, deep distrust and resentment also developed between them. "She accused my parents of being traitors and buying their freedom," explained Tsong, her emotions still running high. "We suffered greatly, as did she, but because she lost her husband and experienced enormous hardships after her arrival, she resents my family and me because we had the resources to rebuild our lives, and she did not."

In spite of her lack of resources, Tsong's mother-in-law managed to put her children through medical school by working a series of menial jobs year after year. Tsong's husband and his sibling, both doctors, also worked very hard, and even though they were given scholarships and fellowships, they both feel a great sense of obligation to their mother. "The woman," said Tsong, "has no life other than her children."

Tsong understands her husband's feelings of obligation to his mother. She, too, feels very close to her parents. "I have never believed that my husband should not feel appreciation toward his mother," she explained. "And because of my husband's show of loyalty toward me, I was able to be

magnanimous to her, in spite of her insults and criticisms."
When forced to choose sides, Tsong's husband's allegiance
never wavered. When his mother made comments that were
clearly offensive to his wife, he always stood up for his wife.

Tsong had a negative relationship with her
mother-in-law that never caused difficulty in her marriage.
Clearly, one can have a good, strong, healthy, and whole-
some marital relationship in spite of a bad mother-in-law/
daughter-in-law relationship, as long as the bond or
"we-ness" between the spouses is firmly grounded. Tsong's
relationship exemplifies how vital the bond between partners
can be. Unlike Sophia, whose husband invalidated her concerns, Tsong's husband asserted healthy boundaries that
reconfirmed the couple's marital strength.

In fact, a real or perceived intrusion by the mother-in-
law, such as Sophia experienced, and its subsequent negation
by the daughter-in-law's spouse, can be the downfall of the
mother-in-law/daughter-in-law relationship and harmful to
the marriage, as well. Fortunately, Tsong's husband's sensitivity to his wife helped her to integrate a disturbing relationship with her mother-in-law. Tsong said, "She does love
our children, so she can't be all that horrible. I figure she
attacks me because she is so limited as a person. She does
know that my children are the most beautiful, brilliant children in the world. At least she knows that!"

Honey, Are You Home?

When Jess' third child was born, which was thirteen years
after her second child, she received less, not more, support
from her husband. "I increasingly felt the need for more of
his time, energy, and physical presence to try to maintain our
schedules, and some semblance of the life we had before the
baby arrived. We needed to renegotiate some basic agree-
ments about various areas of our lives. However, my

husband was limited in the kinds of help he would give me. As the help he chose to give did not meet my needs or those of our children, we had many hard times. My relationship with my mother-in-law also suffered.

"I found that, as my husband was not meeting my needs or the needs of our children, I could no longer go along with satisfying his mother's desires, especially if to do so caused too much juggling of the kids' schedules, or if my husband was unwilling to help out before his folks visited. In the past, I had been very flexible and went out of my way for his family, as I did for mine. Eventually, I ran out of the desire and energy to deal with much other than my immediate family life."

Jess noted that other factors worsened this already difficult predicament. In addition to the loss of her mother and the lack of assistance from her husband, she said, "When my in-laws retired, that affected my relationship with my mother-in-law in a negative way." Since that event, Jess noted a change in her mother-in-law's behavior. "She has become very manipulative. She will not accept 'no' as an answer. Other family members have noticed this, too, but not my husband. If I don't agree with what she wants, my mother-in-law contacts my husband, without saying that she has spoken to me. He then tries to get me to go along with what she wants, which often leads to an argument. It's like dealing with an adolescent who knows how to play the parents against each other. It's hard to put up with and makes me want to avoid all contact with her."

It is clear that Jess is intolerant of her mother-in-law's behavior, and her husband is not. This is the gap that needs to be addressed. Jess and her husband must present a more united front and not allow his mother to be such a divisive force. In addition, Jess needs to make more assertive communications about her concerns, and overcome the retaliatory pitfalls.

Although her situation is totally different from Jess,' Ellen, too, always believed that her husband's allegiance was to his mother and not to her. As she made clear in chapter 2, her mother-in-law adored her and thought she could do no wrong. Because of Ellen's ability to make people feel "as if they were cared for," she always made her mother-in-law feel special. But even the ability to put someone completely at ease is not enough to make a relationship a good one.

Ellen had always felt uncomfortable in her relationship with her mother-in-law. She found many of her mother-in-law's behaviors extremely troublesome. What was most awful for Ellen, however, was her husband's invalidation of her feelings. The tense situation with her mother-in-law was exacerbated by the secondary conflict with her husband, caused by his lack of empathy. What may have been simply annoying became almost unbearable. Her resentment grew and she soon found it hard to have any positive feelings about her mother-in-law.

The striking difference between Ellen and Nancy (see chapter 3) is that Nancy's relationship with her husband was never in jeopardy. Nancy's husband did not place his parents' needs before those of his wife. Personality conflicts aside, both women knew that their mothers-in-law thought they were great daughters-in-law. But Nancy never felt that she was left out in the cold by her husband's relationship with his mother.

Ellen believes that this was not the case with her husband. "When they were alive, my mother-in-law and her husband were very self-absorbed. My husband was a considerate son who never expected much from his parents, but gave generously to them." This became a source of friction between Ellen and Philip. "Philip saw nothing wrong with his parents walking into our home at any time and helping themselves to our wine cellar without asking. Once, when I confronted my mother-in-law with the question, 'Why don't

you come in and say hello before you go down to the basement?' she merely replied that 'they didn't want to forget the
bottles.' She never asked if it was all right to remove those
bottles of wine, or if we might have put some aside for
ourselves.

"My husband said I was wrong to resent their behavior,
and he would not tolerate my criticizing his parents."
Clearly, the sense of "we-ness" that must develop between
couples, if they are to be happy, was not achieved between
this couple (Gottman and Silver 1999). Philip, in effect, shut
out his wife's concerns in defense of his mother.

"I was unable to criticize my mother-in-law in any way.
When I would ask her what they were doing with the wine,
she would just say that she was following her husband." This
repeatedly tense situation brought on tremendous quarrels
between Ellen and Philip. But Ellen still insists that her relationship with her mother-in-law was a good one. She
repeated the fact that she and her mother-in-law were both
artists and enjoyed going out together. They respected each
other's work and complimented one another. Ellen said, "I
suppose it was my distrust and resentment of my father-in-
law that stands out. My mother-in-law wasn't a very strong
woman, so I can't really say that she was the one who made
things so difficult." Nonetheless, Ellen described an event
that was emblematic of her problems with her mother-in-
law's behavior.

"My in-laws retired to Florida after collecting half of
the financial worth of the law firm that my husband, by vir-
tue of his hard work, had developed into a thriving practice
while his parents traveled all around the world and his father
played the horses. In order to pay out to my father-in-law
'his share,' we had to sell our stocks and borrow money!

"Shortly thereafter, they decided to move back to
Detroit, and got a new apartment, and my father-in-law went
back to the law firm from which he once again earned a lot

of money, essentially for not being there. Then, they moved in with us because their new apartment was still being fixed up for them. I had two small children and a 'mother's helper' who was living with us. They displaced my 'mother's helper' from her bedroom. They told her that she should live in the basement for the month or so that they would be living with us. She quit.

"My parents were in South America at the time, so I had no help, two small children, a dog, a cat, and a husband who was putting in ten-hour days at the office. My mother-in-law and father-in-law would wake up, have their breakfast, and leave to meet friends, or look in at their apartment, or buy furniture. . . . They would return at dinner time which they expected that I would have ready for them.

"At no time was any help offered nor any shopping done except for once when my mother-in-law bought four plums, put them in the fridge, and said that her husband would like them and they were for him. After a couple of weeks of this routine, I announced one night that I was exhausted and did not have time to get dinner together. Instead of offering to take us out for dinner, my mother-in-law called up her daughter and invited her out for dinner with them, explaining to her in my hearing that I had not had any dinner prepared. The worse part of this invasion was that my husband would not tolerate my complaining in any way about his mother and father."

Once again, we see that it is the husband's response that made things most difficult. Had Philip been more emotionally connected to Ellen, perhaps she would have felt less resentment of her mother-in-law. In fact, the difficulties, at one point, threatened the stability of the couple's marriage. Unfortunately, Ellen was so injured by her mother-in-law's thoughtlessness that she was unable to respond in a constructive way. She demonstrated a helpless pattern, waiting for her husband's rescue.

Alternatively, Ellen might have been able to persuade her mother-in-law to help around the house and with the child care instead of keeping her at arm's length. This could have served her needs in several ways. While not contradicting her husband's wishes, she might have developed a more collaborative relationship with her mother-in-law. Many women can certainly assert their needs constructively without offending the other party.

Instead, Ellen felt trapped in a never-ending cycle of an unresponsive husband and his exploitive parents. "My in-laws' car was in the shop and my husband decided that they should have my car. He called me from his office and said that they would be over within the hour to pick it up. When I told him that I could not be without my car, he said that he had just spoken to his mother and had promised them my car. There was no reasoning with him, and when he said that I was being hysterical, I called him back and told him that unless he called them back and told them to rent a car, I would do something drastic. He thought I was kidding, and he laughed at me and hung up.

"I turned to my two daughters, then aged eleven and five, and gave them five minutes to pack a bag that included pajamas, bathing suits, and toothbrushes, and to get into the car. I told them we were going to a resort in Pennsylvania. My daughters were curious about the prospect of running away from home. We were lucky enough to get a beautiful room at a resort. This was their first lesson in not allowing themselves to be subjugated by an unreasonably oppressive person even if it was someone whom they loved.

"Because my husband's parents did not find me, my car, or my two daughters when they arrived at our home, they telephoned my husband at the office who, in turn, telephoned my parents who knew nothing about our whereabouts. I later called them to tell them we were safe and in another state. To this day (more than thirty-three years later), my daughters love to tell the story of the time mother ran away from home and took them on the 'great escape.' As for my husband, after I revealed our whereabouts, he drove out to Pennsylvania the next day to retrieve us and apologized to me for his inconsiderate behavior."

What's in a Daughter?

Kelsey is another woman who receives little or no help from her husband when it comes to her troubled relationship with her mother-in-law. She thinks that her husband is often blind to his mother's behavior. Unlike Nel, whose mother-in-law had no daughters, and who made a special place in her heart for Nel, Kelsey's mother-in-law was not ready to let another woman into her life with her sons.

Most of the women interviewed for this book whose husbands had no sisters were accepted by their mothers-in-law as "the daughter" they never had. There were, however, some glaring exceptions. Arnstein, in her 1985 book, described finding that the absence of a daughter in the mother-in-law's family made the adjustment of becoming a mother-in-law more difficult than for those mothers-in-law who had daughters, and were more familiar with this relationship. Perhaps it was this lack of "daughter experience" that contributed to the problems that Kelsey has with her mother-in-law.

Kelsey admits, "My mother-in-law and I have an extremely complicated relationship. When I first met my husband, I was sixteen. I was from a really marginalized family situation: early divorce, many years of poverty, drug and alcohol abuse by both parents, subsequent marriages and divorces. Lots of wishing I had had a 'normal' childhood with college-educated, financially solvent parents. When I met Alexander and was accepted by his family, I thought I had struck gold."

Kelsey had had hopes of a special connection with her mother-in-law since there were only sons in her husband's family. "I thought we'd be pals and I'd be the daughter she never had, honestly." Kelsey found that what you see isn't always what you get. "They seemed to have everything I lacked, a strong, responsible family of smart people who loved each other. Though there had been a divorce, it had been the only one, and the family still seemed fairly intact, which was enviable. I thought Alex's mom was wonderful—so smart and so cultured and so warm to me."

The difficulties that Kelsey eventually faced were much more intense than simply not getting along with her mother-in-law. But what was most troubling in her day-to-day life was that she did not have her husband's support. The wives of her husband's brothers had similar complaints, Kelsey said. "None of the daughters-in-law feel our husbands protect us from her. Everyone has to coddle her and see to it that her every wish is granted."

Kelsey admits that things did change some after her son was born. Although she believes that her mother-in-law has no real love for her, she does feel that her husband's mother, in moments of "clarity and awareness when she is not feeling paranoid or defensive," sees Kelsey's positive influences. "She would say that things are not easy between us, but that she thinks I'm a wonderful mother and that her son loves me very much."

Unlike Kelsey, Hope said of her relationship with her mother-in-law, "I wouldn't be surprised if she thought of me as a daughter or said she did. After all, I don't think she has any true or intimate connections with her own daughter or her other daughters-in-law."

Hope said, "I mean, the longest conversation I have ever had with my mother-in-law that did not involve my daughter was about what color stuffed animal she was going to give to each of her daughters-in-law. She was very happy to have gotten these free stuffed animals from some church function and it seemed to consume much of her time and energy picking which one should go with which daughter-in-law. I don't ever remember seeing her so animated. It was weird. When my uncle died last year, the only contact my mother-in-law made to my father was a Hallmark card with her name signed at the bottom. She didn't even include a personal note. She probably sent Hallmark cards to her own daughter when she had her baby."

Clearly, being "like a daughter" does not guarantee an idyllic maternal bond for a daughter-in-law. The role of "daughter" is as idiosyncratic as the role of "daughter-in-law," or any other family role.

Bad Break

What we found most extraordinary about the stories in Part I, chapters 1 through 3 (The Good), and Part II, chapters 4 through 6 (The Bad), was that many of the issues of the mother-in-law/daughter-in-law relationship described by the daughters-in-law were often the same or very similar. But the tools the women used to handle their relationships and the way they interpreted certain actions of their mothers-in-law were different.

What distinguished the "good" from the "bad" was not the content of the behaviors, but how the daughters-in-law acted upon it. In chapters 1 through 3 (The Good), daughters-in-law thought they had good relationships when they were able and willing to negotiate terrain that was not easy. Those daughters-in-law worked at maintaining the positive aspects of their relationships and also worked on improving the more difficult parts of relating to their mothers-in-law. They repaired ruptures when they occurred.

In chapters 4 through 6 (The Bad), many of the daughters-in-law were either unable or unwilling to exercise constructive communication with their mothers-in-law. Because of fear, hurt, passivity, pessimistic thinking, or a host of other reasons, many of these daughters-in-law did not even open up the subject for discussion, let alone work their problems through with their mothers-in-law or spouses.

Frequently, these daughters-in-law externalized blame. They did not see themselves as instrumental or agents of change who could develop healthier relationships. Often we found a learned helplessness when the spouse was the focal point. The condition of learned helplessness was exacerbated when the spousal relationship was unsupportive. When the spouse saw himself as caught between his mother and his wife, his wife often felt offended when asked to consider her mother-in-law's side at all. The daughter-in-law felt betrayed. Many of the daughters-in-law in these chapters felt abandoned by their life partners with whom they have not formed truly autonomous relationships.

Furthermore, daughters-in-law, such as Sharon, who felt bound and gagged by the needs of decorum and politeness above authentic expression, tended to let their problems fester. Now, they harbor negative feelings that seem insurmountable. Those who tended to resent and brood allowed this dysfunction within their mother-in-law relationship to endanger their marriages.

Throughout chapters 4 through 6 (The Bad) we see little to no evidence of either party trying to make things better or considering a search for outside help. This passive stance will not ease feelings. The ill will grows and perpetuates a chronically dissatisfying relationship. This disharmony does not reside in a vacuum. It has an impact on the family in small and large ways. A couple is faced with a tremendous journey. Together they encounter a web of complex relationships. As they begin to create a family, they must address their individual histories and their present relationships with their families of origin.

Sometimes, families can intrude on a marriage, depleting it rather than bolstering it. The struggle of balancing different family traditions can get in the way of creating new ones. A woman may reject a tradition because she resents the mother-in-law who observes it. Or she may reject the mother-in-law because she finds the tradition not to her liking. These conflicts become symbolic of survival. The daughter-in-law may develop an armor of defenses, insisting on matters that are not important in themselves but that may be imbued with symbolic significance. She must wrestle with the deeper issues if transformation is to occur.

Where Do You Go from Here?

1. **Get support.** If you are not ready or you are unable to talk to your mother-in-law, get support elsewhere. You need a safe environment to surmount your struggles. If you are worried that this cannot be readily achieved, seek professional help.

2. **Begin to discuss some of your concerns with your husband.** Enlist his input in how best to address the issues with your mother-in-law.

3. **Practice assertive communication skills in less tense relationships.** Find other people with whom you can investigate ways of communicating. Learn how to say what you feel without attacking the other person.

4. **Enhance this relationship in another dimension.** Take some time to generate or build on the positive things. Fan the flames of "like," not "dislike." Remember, this woman is your husband's mother and, unless there is true pathology, attempts should be make to make things work as well as possible. Having a relationship is better than not.

5. **Get to know her.** Daughters-in-law frequently lament that their mothers-in-law don't know them. Ask yourself if that dynamic goes both ways. Take the initiative and model curiosity. Find out what she likes and doesn't, what she believes and doesn't.

6. **Give credence to the culture clash.** Some differences may be neutral, yet feel "shockingly terrible" just because they are unfamiliar. Don't let the differences create schisms. Try to make room for them.

7. **Did she really mean to hurt you?** Create a list of alternative explanations for your mother-in-law's perceived negative actions. Consider biases, such as culture, generation, religion, and so on. Also, sometimes, kindness has a strange way of showing itself. Could shey have offended when she meant to help?

8. **Be thoughtful about what you communicate to your children.** Unless it is to protect them from jeopardy, keep the issues between you and your mother-in-law away from them. If there are difficulties between the two of you and she is still a wonderful grandmother, don't risk tainting their relationship. Unlike your spouse, your kids should not have to choose sides.

9. **You are not wrong to feel sensitive.** There is a unique vulnerability that goes along with being a daughter-in-law. You are bonded to someone who has been bonded to someone else for a lifetime. Be aware of your sensitivity. Try to monitor and regulate your emotional reactivity. However, don't shut down to protect yourself. Try to convey ideas that invoke deeper issues or sensitivities. Let each other in.

10. **Recognize the symbolism.** You may find yourself feeling outraged or overreacting to something small. Don't listen to advice that tells you your complaints are petty and to ignore them. Certainly, you want to gain some perspective. But see things for what they really are. This means finding out what else is involved in your struggle. Try to get to the heart of the matter.

11. **Expand the listening process.** When negotiating a solution, avoid condemnation and nagging. You are not the teacher or the parent. Communicate feelings about yourself. Listen and restate to make sure you understand what your mother-in-law or spouse is communicating.

12. **There is no recipe that works for everyone.** We have seen how similar issues can produce very different outcomes, depending on how a relationship is approached. What you decide to do must be congruent with who you are. Trying to modify your own or your mother-in-law's behavior to the point where everyone is behaving unnaturally would not be productive. Don't try to change who you are and don't expect your mother-in-law to do that either. Try to be positive and do not assume the worst. Don't give up . . . yet.

13. **While being careful not to put yourself somewhere that is emotionally unsafe, try to think about what can make this relationship better.** Resignation is fatal to the promise of a better relationship. Don't throw in the towel.

Part III: The Ugly
She was horrid!

Chapter 7

Unforgivable?

From Day One she made it clear that she disapproved of me and I should keep my distance. We first met in a restaurant and she assumed I had never been to an expensive restaurant before, and that I wouldn't know how to read a posh menu. She thought she had to help me read it, and she sneered at me while she read it aloud. . . . It's hard, even if you know that your mother-in-law is wrong, to feel great about yourself when you are constantly being told you're not good enough.

—Mariette

Because I was not "English" (although I was born in London and my mother was English), and my husband and I didn't get married in the Church of England, we were just not accepted. My mother-in-law believed that her family was of a much higher class than mine.

—Ursula

I was in tears. We were riding the train home from somewhere, I don't remember. But I do remember that Kim stood up and took my hand, and said to his mother, "I will not ride in the same car with anyone who treats my wife with such disrespect."

—Tsong

"Ugly," as a description, doesn't beat around the bush. Subjective to some degree, it is less vague than "good" or "bad," leaving less to the imagination. In Part III we will examine relationships that have become or always were, to a large degree, hopeless. This is not to say that we will revert to stereotypical mother-in-law jokes and find truth behind the cruel humor.

Mothers-in-law, like lawyers and other maligned figures in society, are just people and they come in as many shapes and sizes as the rest of us. They come from all walks of life, all kinds of backgrounds, and exemplify as many different kinds of personalities as exist on the planet. The one thing all mothers-in-law have in common is that they have a child who now has a spouse.

The relationships in chapters 7, 8, and 9 do not inspire compassion for the mother-in-law. Here are situations from which great pain resulted, usually for all the parties involved. In Part II, we often could comprehend and accept the behavior of both the mother-in-law and the daughter-in-law. Generally, we could either empathize with or understand how those mothers-in-law could come to feel or behave in the ways they did. However, when extreme behavior results in equally extreme damage, it is difficult not to judge the person whose behavior caused the damage.

Behavior That Hurts

No relationship is without its moments of insensitivity or thoughtless action. In the preceding chapters, you saw how certain behaviors of mothers-in-law cause distress for their daughter-in-laws. But even in Part II, the "bad" section, the hurtful behavior was often accidental or not extreme. In other words, the hurtful behaviors described in Part II were mostly forgivable. In Part III, you will find examples of extreme behaviors that seem unforgivable.

For example, Mariette, the interior designer, whom you first met in chapter 1, felt that, initially, she might not survive her mother-in-law's extremely cold behavior. During Mariette's engagement and the first few years of her marriage, her mother-in-law alienated her. Fortunately, the birth of her twin girls dramatically changed her relationship with her husband's mother for the better.

When Mariette remembered how she had been treated by her mother-in-law before her children were born, she said, "From day one she made it clear that she disapproved of me and I should keep my distance. We first met in a restaurant and she assumed I had never been to an expensive restaurant before, and that I wouldn't know how to read a posh menu. She thought she had to help me read it, and she sneered at me while she read it aloud. When we told her that we were engaged to be married, she stopping talking to me. She even stopped making eye contact with me."

After that dinner, Mariette's future mother-in-law proceeded to do everything she could to sabotage the impending marriage. For example, Mariette and her then fiancé, Devon, were commanded to visit his mother's house in Worcester every weekend. Mariette made the two-hour-long trip from Boston several times, only to be greeted with a cold shoulder at each visit. Devon's mother went so far as to serve Mariette bread crusts and potato peels, with the explanation that there simply wasn't enough food to offer her anything else, but that "these were really the best parts, anyway." After the second of such "meals," Mariette had enough. She told Devon that she would no longer visit his mother with him. He did not disagree with her. Later, he chose to stay with Mariette many weekends, and when he wanted to visit his mother, he made the trip alone.

Mariette's mother-in-law never lost an opportunity to let Mariette know that she thought Mariette was "white trash." "My mother-in-law made it very clear she did not want to socialize with my parents. This hurt and offended them and me." Mariette noted that her family, although not wealthy, is well educated and very involved in community activities.

Her mother-in-law did everything she could to cast Mariette in a negative light to prove to her son that he would be making a big mistake if he chose Mariette as his wife. Seventeen years later, Devon and Mariette's marriage is the strongest it has ever been. "I think our earlier trials with my husband's mother actually strengthened our marriage," said Mariette. "It was very difficult for both of us; like we survived the war together."

When the couple proved to be a united, impenetrable pair, they positioned his mother as the clear outsider. They let her know by their actions that it was she who had to fit into their world. Thus, it finally became clear to Mariette's mother-in-law that hostile behavior would only alienate her further and, ultimately, leave her more alone.

In the years that followed the birth of her twin daughters, Mariette found her relationship with her mother-in-law had stabilized and actually became positive in many ways. "We take long walks together and talk," marveled Mariette. "This would have been unthinkable for both of us five years ago. We've actually become good friends. Her new boyfriend told me she gushes compliments about me! Could this be true?

"Recently, on one of our walks, my mother-in-law told me that it was a good thing that I hadn't been a smoker when she met me, because, if I had been a smoker, I'd have been 'Out of here.' There was a time when I would have been enraged by the idea that she felt she had 'veto power' over her son's choices. Now I just bite my tongue when she says something horrid. And I always have to giggle to myself because when she met me I *did* smoke!"

Tsong, whom you met in chapter 6, also feels that certain things redeem her mother-in-law and prevent what was in many ways "bad" from turning into a truly ugly relationship. "Once my mother-in-law accused my parents of being outright collaborators in the old country. She had always hinted that she believed they escaped by buying their way out, but she had never before said it to my face. I was in tears. We were riding the train home from somewhere, I don't remember. But I do remember that Kim stood up and took my hand, and said to his mother, 'I will not ride in the same car with anyone who treats my wife with such disrespect.' He led me out and we rode in another car. I never heard another evil word from her regarding my parents."

Things That Cannot Be Unsaid

We've often heard, "You can't take it back." That's because words can wound much more deeply than sticks or stones. We can recover from bruises, but the damage done to our sense of self may never recover from cruelties spoken either carelessly or said in anger, with the intent to hurt.

Portia was born on the island of Martinique and raised in Paris. She speaks seven languages, and holds a master's degree in sociology. ("West Indians are terrible over-achievers. It's in our blood," she noted.) She and her husband, Nikos, run their own business. They met in graduate school in London. He is from rural Greece and was the only one from his family, which includes six siblings, to attend college. When Portia and her husband were engaged, she tried to impress her future mother-in-law when she came to London for a visit. "I cooked a fabulous meal and she didn't look at me the entire time," she remembered. "A week after she returned to Greece, Nikos received a letter from her and it made him cry, so I insisted on seeing it. She told Nikos that she thought I was a horrible woman. He cried some more. It was terrible. But we loved each other and tried to rise above it." Portia spent several years being referred to as "that woman." Once, when Nikos returned from visiting his parents, Nikos and Portia found a talisman hidden among his underwear, "protecting" him from his wife, "the black devil."

Kadijah also lives in London, but was born in Jordan. She moved to the U.K. to attend medical school, and she is now a doctor. Kadijah identifies herself as an Arab Muslim. In her case, she never felt that her mother-in-law had ever had any respect for her because she was never once treated respectfully. It also became clear early in her marriage that her mother-in-law was not shy of belittling her in front of others.

"When my mother-in-law came to visit us in London," she said, "she bought me a gift. It was a lovely bracelet. I was very surprised. She put the bracelet on my wrist, keeping hold of it. Then, she said, 'Oh, your arm is too skinny for this lovely bracelet,' and she took it back and put it on her daughter's wrist. Clearly, she had wanted to *appear* to give me something. But she never gave me anything. Ever. She was always doing things like that.

"She would look at my nightgown and make remarks about how sluttish it was. She called me a whore because my mother was a Jordanian. In her mind, all Jordanian women were whores. Before we married, she prayed five times a day that her son would not marry a Jordanian. This is aside from the fact that she married a Jordanian herself. Go figure."

Second-Class Citizen

A woman can be made to feel inferior by her mother-in-law and allow herself to submit to the status of a second-class citizen without even realizing it. Sometimes, a daughter-in-law feels shame for allowing herself to be trapped in abusive mother-in-law/daughter-in-law exchanges. She may feel completely demoralized by the nature of the relationship. Often, too, she may feel that no escape is possible. The insecurity that is generated may bleed into her spousal relationship. The daughter-in-law may start to feel unwanted by all or worry (sometimes correctly) that her husband will begin to share his mother's biases.

When Portia stayed at her mother-in-law's home in the Greek countryside, she felt trapped. She said, "Several years ago, this awful incident took place during my last visit to my mother-in-law's house. One evening I had gone upstairs to put my son to bed. When I came back downstairs and walked into the kitchen-dining room, I saw a couple, friends of my in-law's, I had never met before had come to visit. As I walked into the room, everyone except my mother-in-law looked up, and the room became silent.

"Nobody said a word as I walked through the room to take a seat. The awkward silence continued while the couple waited to find out who 'this strange woman' was. Finally, my father-in-law said to the man, 'Have you ever met my son Nikos' wife?' and then he made the introductions. My mother-in-law, who had been conversing with the woman, simply turned away and ignored me. She refused even to acknowledge my presence to her guest. She was clearly very embarrassed by me. The woman and I exchanged sheepish smiles and nods, and I continued to sit there feeling like a nasty, dark stain on a white sheet until the visit was over. I swore then that I would never set foot in that house again."

Portia noted that the incident was also awkward for her husband, Nikos, and that it had made trouble between the two of them. But she had been able to see his position. "My husband was in the room that evening, and he did not introduce me either. At the time I was very angry with him, and I felt that he had abandoned me. But he explained that he had been waiting to see his parents do the right thing. And I thought that this was the correct thing to do. He has always given them the opportunity to do the right thing, and has always believed that it is just a matter of time before my mother-in-law comes around. He's much more of an optimist than I am."

Mariette, too, tried to be understanding, but she had reached her tolerance threshold. "There's only so much abuse someone can take," she said. "At some point, my life had become so miserable around his mother that I just refused to go to her house anymore. She had been insisting that we come over every Sunday for dinner. Actually, she was insisting that *he* should come every Sunday, and he asked me to accompany him. When I finally said I had had enough, he didn't push it.

"One Sunday, though, Devon was really sick. He was running a high fever and his mother still insisted that he come over, because she didn't want to eat Sunday dinner alone. Also, she always assumed that we lied about everything, and that he wasn't really sick or that we really didn't have any other plans. Anyway, that night I was not going to support the craziness of driving for two hours to Worcester and I didn't think he should either. But he did. This really struck me hard. I felt at that point that Devon needed some help. He finally spoke to his stepmother about the issue and she had great advice for him.

His stepmother, Florence, simply told Devon that he is *not* responsible for his mother's life and that he *is* responsible for his own and for our life together. What a relief! I still think that our decision to move to Florida was greatly, very greatly, influenced by his mother's proximity. Boston was a bit too close to her. Moving was a good decision. I was able to feel whole outside of her radar. I was able to, well, really feel good about myself again. It's hard, even if you know that your mother-in-law is wrong, to feel great about yourself when you are constantly being told you're not good enough."

Ursula, who is a vocal coach in West Yorkshire, England, received the same kind of contempt from her mother-in-law. Ursula said that she had been so young when she married, she had no idea what she was getting into, and she didn't even grasp the extent to which she was put down by her mother-in-law. "We grew up on the same street, went to the same schools," she said of her husband and herself, "but we were brought up in very different households. I was brought up Catholic and my husband was Church of England. For his family, this meant we were worlds apart. I was often told by my mother-in-law that my father was just an Irish laborer (he was an engineer), and I was married to the son of a barrister and should respect the class difference and recognize how lucky I had been to marry above my station. Because I was not 'English' (although I was born in London and my mother was English), and my husband and I didn't get married in the Church of England, we were just not accepted. My mother-in-law believed that her family was of a much higher class than mine.

"My father was a nine-to-five 'Irish immigrant,' and her husband was a barrister, a wealthy businessman, *and* a member of the House of Lords. According to his mother, a Lord's son was not made to follow rules like other people. My husband was expected to follow in his father's footsteps, so he had little incentive to go out on his own and stand up for anything. That's a lot to hand over to a teenager and expect to help him become a man.

"I never truly complained to my husband about his mother. I was so desperate to please her. My mother-in-law always would say to me, 'You can do whatever you want to in your marriage, as long as you don't upset your husband.' I often wondered how far this extended. This was, in any case, a difficult rule for me to follow. My husband and I worked together and I still had the voice coaching. I could do as I pleased, but only if I found a baby-sitter, cleaned the house, and took care of everything so as not upset my husband. This went on for twenty-five years.

"I don't think it was unusual for women to be treated this way, especially in their class, but that didn't make it right. I was treated as, and believed myself to be, a second-class citizen. She would serve the Christmas dinner and I would serve the Boxing Day meal. We would call mine the 'Irish' dinner and hers the 'Proper English' dinner. At the time I found that acceptable, but now I know it was a snub.

"I was never made to feel that I was a part of the family or that I even belonged. One afternoon I was sitting with my mother-in-law and sister-in-law. My sister-in-law made a remark about my mother-in-law's lovely broach, a pink cameo that I had given her for Mother's Day perhaps two weeks before. 'Where did you get such a lovely broach?' my sister-in-law asked. 'It's something I picked up somewhere,' she answered. After my sister-in-law left the table, I asked 'Why didn't you tell her that I gave that to you?' She answered, 'Because she didn't give me anything and I didn't want her feelings to get hurt.' There was never regard for my feelings. I had hoped that, as I gained recognition in my mother-in-law's church circle that that would please her. I always felt I was still the 'neighbor's girl,' never her daughter-in-law.

"Once, while my husband was in school and I was working for the railroad as a payroll officer, I had to bring the paychecks home for the weekend. I placed them carefully in a drawer in my room in the basement. I was running errands and I came home to find my mother-in-law holding all of the payroll checks and accusing me of stealing. My sister-in-law, who was eleven, had been going through the drawers and brought them up to her. I thought, 'What am I doing here explaining myself when she'd been going through my private things?' I wondered if she'd been through my knickers' drawer as well."

Summary Questions

Everyone has a different pain threshold. Some things become water under the bridge. Other things remain dammed.

* *Think of another relationship, prior to this, that had a negative impact on your life. How does that one compare to your current relationship with your mother-in-law?*

* *Do you identify with anyone in this chapter? If not, how would you handle any of these relationships?*

* *In objective terms (use the third person "she"), describe your relationship with your mother-in-law in a paragraph. Read your story aloud and then offer advice.*

Chapter 8

The Pain and the Damage Done

She clings to a self-image that she's a nice old lady who likes to read books and give money to her children, and that she has "terrific" (her word) relationships with her daughters-in-law, but really she's a maniac, waiting in the shadows with a sharp knife, ready for the attack. I feel sorry for her because she's so clueless about how to help herself. She's so deluded.

—Kelsey

In my husband's family, wives were nothing. The children, the siblings, were exclusively entitled. When his father died, my mother-in-law took over. She was truly the matriarch—the Grand Dame. She rejected all of her children's spouses and took control of the grandchildren. She still rules from the grave.

—Ursula

In previous chapters, you read about ways in which a daughter-in-law might be able to improve her relationship with her mother-in-law by coming to accept her and making room for her in her life. Sometimes, however, wounds cannot be healed so easily; sometimes, they cannot be healed at all. It takes a woman as magnanimous as Mariette or Tsong to accept such deep hurt and continue to relate to her mother-in-law. But such acceptance also requires having a strong bond with your husband. "Gong Ching" in Mandarin refers to the bond shared through experience (Yuan 2000). Often, this experience, when traumatic, can create a more intense bond.

Such a strong bond creates an equally strong foundation upon which the daughter-in-law can stand securely against the insults or dysfunctional behaviors that may be present in her relationship with her mother-in-law. Without such a bond with her husband, a woman may feel that her marriage, as well as her relationship with her mother-in-law, is somehow in peril. Preparing to spend a lifetime with a mother-in-law who creates friction in your life and spews anger at you is a huge challenge. Confidence in your spouse to help you deal with such hardship is of utmost importance. You should not be expected to weather such a storm alone.

How Could You Have Known?

In relationships that have been damaged severely or that now seem truly hopeless, the warning signs of terrible things to come may not have been recognizable. Sometimes, there are no warning signs at all. For example, Kelsey, whom you met in chapter 6, had strong positive feelings about her mother-in-law at the beginning, but she soon found that the relationship was going to be impossible. Over the years, she discovered that the problem was greater than two women just not getting along.

Kelsey said, "Over the last sixteen years I've learned that she is mentally ill. I've learned the hard way, from her raging at me, or not speaking to me over tiny missteps. It became clear to me that my mother-in-law once experienced a profound trauma in her life, which continues to bear down on the family, it is a burden on everyone. She's a fanatic perfectionist and her control freak behavior is prone to shame-based raging.

"My mother-in-law is also incredibly hermit-like and has trained the family to follow suit. Her motto is, 'Don't trust anyone outside of the family.' Including daughters-in-law, and there are four of us. We've all had our share of Draca trying to turn our husbands, or each other, against us. Anything can trigger her feelings of humiliation, which then incites her anger. And when she gets mad, everyone feels her wrath. It's been known to wreck family gatherings.

"One Christmas she got so angry at me that I left the house in tears while Alexander yelled at her for being mean to me. She clings to a self-image that she's a nice old lady who likes to read books and give money to her children, and that she has 'terrific' (her word) relationships with her daughters-in-law, but really she's a maniac, waiting in the shadows with a sharp knife, ready for the attack. I feel sorry for her because she's so clueless about how to help herself. She's so deluded. Recently I told my sister-in-law that I realized that whatever Draca says, she really means the opposite. 'I just love my daughters-in-law' translated means 'I can't believe what a bunch of losers my sons married.' 'I really believe in total honesty—I'd rather hear the truth and know where you're coming from than make believe everything's fine.' This translates as, 'Say one thing I disagree with, and I'll cut your ovaries out of your body and have them for tea.'"

Kelsey is sure that unless her mother-in-law seeks psychiatric help, there is little chance of anything changing.

Because Draca is her husband's mother, Kelsey thinks that she would be willing to make more of an effort to get along with her, but not if matters remain as they are. "To be frank I wish my mother-in-law would investigate the possibility of medication for her anxiety and social phobias. I realize this puts the onus completely on her to change, but I can't really see the relationship improving while she is so mentally unstable.

"Alexander and I have very strained interactions when it comes to his mother. She's so oversensitive and so anxious that she's constantly commenting on how things are going with all three of us. And she's very protective of Alexander. This is the messy part of my marriage, and it has taken me years even to find the vocabulary to talk about it. Now we more or less know what we're getting ourselves into and we try to join together before we visit her. But that's not always possible. Alexander sometimes has a hard time staying in the moment when we're together. She's so overwhelming that sometimes he just checks out. This drives me crazy, because I need him to be my partner when we're around her, and he's not capable of it at those times."

At this point, however, Kelsey feels that she has come a long way and is standing on firmer ground. "I've grown up a lot in the sixteen years I've known her," said Kelsey with confidence. "I can face myself and her with a lot more clarity. Our relationship had been more or less in decline until Alex and I had our son. Now we all have clearer roles with each other, and I feel more empowered to express myself when I'm irritated with her, and also not to engage with her if I choose to do that."

Kadijah noted that, although there were many interactions between her mother-in-law and herself before she married, she didn't see her husband's mother's early behavior as ruinous to her marriage. "Initially, our two families were friends," she said. "They had a long relationship before our marriage that went back forty years. The two families used to get along well. Surprisingly, my husband and I were born in the same place, in the same country, even in the same hospital. So, many of our childhood experiences were very similar. We knew one another all our lives. I must admit that even when I was a child, I never liked my mother-in-law. I was never comfortable around her."

Dysfunctional from the Start

Knowing what you are going to face is surely preferable to not knowing But just knowing may not prepare you for what lies ahead. When a woman marries someone whose mother is truly mentally ill and whose pathology impinges on others negatively, she must brace herself for profound challenges ahead. Kadijah saw both signs and behavior that she recognized as indicators of future problems. "Because I knew this woman for years, I had very low expectations," she said. "I would have liked for us to be able to communicate better, but I did not expect it. Neither did I expect the intensity of her disrespect for me; but it was not a surprise. That, of course, does not mean it was not hurtful.

"As I said, I never liked her. I have known her since I was a girl of seven. She was never nice to me, not ever. She served old food to us kids. She served us moldy or moth-eaten cookies. She thought that we (my mother and I) were not good enough for the food that she served herself. She was not poor, by any means. This was not an oversight. It was an intentional slight and she made it clear by not eating the same food that she served to us. What civilized person would do such a thing? Such behavior! I always saw her as a withholding, unhappy, obsessive woman."

Ursula, like Kadijah, knew her mother-in-law from childhood. She said, "I was married at the age of nineteen, and I was married for twenty-five years before divorcing. My

first husband and I lived at his mother's house for the first
six months of our marriage. My mother-in-law had English
and Scottish parents and was raised Church of England. Her
husband was a barrister and a member of the House of
Lords. She was from a farming family and lived in her husband's shadow. I do believe that she was abused by him. My
sister-in-law picked up on this when she was a child and she
would say things to her mother like, 'You're nothing but a
peasant, you're good for nothing but scrubbing floors and
milking cows.' It was horrid.

"Even when things were at their worst between us, I
still spoke to her with respect. My husband became just like
his father. He was fabulous in Parliament, but he was like
Dr. Jekyl and Mr. Hyde. He was a tyrant at home. He
became a carbon copy of his father, even though he had not
wanted that to happen.

"In my husband's family, wives were nothing. The children, the siblings, were exclusively entitled. When his father
died, my mother-in-law took over. She was truly the matriarch—the Grand Dame. She rejected all of her children's
spouses and took control of the grandchildren. She still rules
from the grave. Her children never learned to be responsible
for themselves. My husband never made a decision or move
without his mother's approval. My consent or advice was
never asked. This was definitely part of the downfall of our
relationship."

Mariette received a similar cold welcome from her
mother-in-law. Mariette said, "Devon's mother disapproved
of me from the very start. She didn't like anything about me,
she didn't even like the state I came from. She thought she
knew what a woman from a working-class, Quebecoise family was like. Heck, I wasn't even a 'real' Canadian. When I
was 'invited' to her house for dinner, I literally was fed
scraps. It wasn't even that she wanted Devon to have all the
good stuff. She figured, that I, being of low standards and

lower class, wouldn't notice and would be pleased with whatever I got."

Portia, too, was greeted with coldness when she married. She said, "The difference in life experience between my parents and my husband's parents was the bigger factor. Recently, I've been thinking about my upbringing along class lines. There wasn't a lot of money when I was a child, and I come from a one-parent, female-headed household, but both of my parents came from middle/upper-middle-class homes. When my father left us, our financial situation took a nose dive because, at my father's insistence, my mother had never worked during her marriage. So she could only get unskilled, poorly paid jobs, and my father paid no alimony. But the expectations and customs within our family were still solidly middle class (e.g., educational achievement was prized, attending college was expected, and reading and travel were encouraged).

"On the other hand, my husband's birth family was intact, and both his parents were working class, hailing from rural backgrounds where they worked as children on their parents' farms. No one in his family went as far in school as both my father and mother did. But his family members all worked and they saved up enough to become homeowners. They enjoyed a relatively good standard of living. However they are much 'simpler' folk than my comparatively sophisticated parents."

Ugly in the Eye

Ugliness, like beauty, can sometimes exist only in the eye of the beholder. As stated at the beginning of this book, the categories "good," "bad," or "ugly" depend on how the daughter-in-law defines her relationship to her mother-in-law. Often, it is the way a daughter-in-law views the relationship, and her reactions and response to her mother-in-law's actions, that determine whether the relationship is in need of help, or whether it is beyond help. If a daughter-in-law *feels* tortured by her mother-in-law, she will see and define the relationship as tortuous.

For some other women, however, what the rest of the world may think of as "not-so-bad," might be wholly unacceptable. This can happen because of unattainably high standards or because of a dysfunctional undercurrent not visible to the outsider's eye. Generally, "ugly" stands on its own and rears its head.

Ugly on Trial

Fawn, an entrepreneur who runs a business from her home, believes that her mother-in-law is out to get her. Although she feels that she is an uninvited outsider, she also feels that she is being pulled into commitments she would rather avoid. "My mother-in-law never 'asks' us to dinner, or a holiday. She always *commands* us to come, with a complete disregard that we are trying to have a life. If I say we can't, because we're committed already, she hangs up on me!" Fawn resents this intrusive behavior, but she thinks it is unavoidable. Her husband feels the need to acquiesce.

"What's so weird is that she is unsupportive of her son or 'our' family," Fawn said. "My husband never felt loved by his mother so he's stuck in his intense obsession of trying to please her and win her approval. His dad died right when he got out of high school, and he was sent away to boarding school when he was really young, so his mother could pursue her career. He never got the mother-love he always craved. And he's still craving it. My family wasn't perfect, but, for the most part, everyone was nurturing. I put my own kids first and, even though I run a business, I make sure that my children know I am here for them. My mother-in-law never, ever did this for her kids."

Fawn was married once before. "My first marriage lasted two years. That mother-in-law was very nice. We got along great. It's not the mother-in-law thing that is difficult. It's *this* mother-in-law. At first, I thought I would actually enjoy knowing her since she is a very bright woman and speaks several languages. She's an art historian and I thought, since my business is creating a forum for artists on the Internet, that we'd have something to share. I couldn't have been more wrong."

Fawn believes that her mother-in-law has deliberately tried to alienate her and push her away. "She gives me a Christmas presents signed 'From L. Hawthorne.' It's as if she was signing her check!" Fawn feels that the relationship is totally hopeless and not worth trying to salvage. She interprets her mother-in-law's actions as driven by malice and dislike. "I'm sure she thinks nasty things about me. It gets worse each year, as I refuse to participate in the activities she plans for me and my husband."

But her husband's need for his mother's approval is the most troubling aspect of the relationship, and the issue that Fawn finds the hardest to face. She feels his need for his mother's love trumps any of their own family's needs. "Sometimes I can't believe we're still married," she admitted. "It gets so bad I feel like I can't take it anymore. One year, she commanded my husband to come to Prague for Christmas with her and the family. This was when our first daughter was two. My daughter was born with infantile arthritis, so I knew I didn't want my husband to travel out of town with this child, much less to travel out of the country! Being alone with our little girl was not something I wanted either. But my husband felt so obligated to his mother, he went! He was gone for fourteen days, leaving me and Wendy to fend for ourselves! I thought about divorce all the time he was gone."

The degree to which Fawn feels alienated by her husband, because of his need for his mother's acceptance, is unbearable to Fawn. She refuses all interactions with her mother-in-law and resents her husband's opposing needs. His behavior reinforces the importance of a unified front between the partners in this marriage. What is "ugly" here, although it may not seem so ugly compared to other ugly scenarios discussed in these pages, is not what Fawn's mother-in-law does, as much as what Fawn and her spouse do not do. If a couple could arrive at a deeper understanding of the issues they face, and the triangulations that result from those issues, their marriage might stand a better chance of succeeding.

Summary Questions

❋ *Do differences in how you and your husband were raised affect your relationship with your mother-in-law? If so, how do these differences function in your relationship?*

❋ *If you are a mother, do you and your mother-in-law have different approaches to child rearing? If so, how do these different practices impact on your relationship?*

Chapter 9

Negotiating the
Chasm

*We went out to see some friends and when we
returned to his mother's house, she had left a
note on Devon's pillow that said, she "felt that
I should leave, and he should stay." ... It was
the middle of the night and I was not going to
stay in her house another minute. I told Devon
I was leaving. That was the big moment. He
said, "I'm coming with you." And we left his
mother's house together. After this, she began to
realize that she could not control Devon's life.
He and I were a couple and she could not
come between us.*

—Mariette

*When I divorced her son, she declared me dead.
She wanted to bury me after the divorce. In a
way she did, symbolically; she told my kids,
"You don't have a mother anymore. She died."*

—Ursula

Once a daughter-in-law acknowledges that she and her mother-in-law will not have an ideal relationship, she can begin to take steps toward creating a better situation. This chapter includes information that may help with damage control. Many of the issues described by daughters-in-law in this chapter cause irreparable damage to a marriage and must be addressed if the marriage is to be saved.

Unbreakable Marriage

Like a healthy organism, a marriage cannot endure significant obstacles and stressors if it is not fundamentally sound. The partners must feel a strong bond and a sense of cohesion, described as the state of "we-ness" in earlier chapters. Even when there is such a strong bond, one partner may exhibit a certain carelessness that can cause the other partner to feel that the bond has been breached. A woman who feels that her husband is not honoring their partnership may also feel that the marriage is in jeopardy, however insignificant the breach may seem to the husband.

Mariette admitted that the situation with her mother-in-law had caused severe problems in her marriage. "Things with Devon were pretty hard. He would acknowledge that his mother was mistreating me, but he kept asking me to be patient. He kept reminding me how pathetic her life was and that she had no one but him. This didn't help me, but I tried to be generous. I hated adding to his misery. He really didn't know what to do. He felt terribly guilty and beholden unto his mother. You see, his mother didn't raise him. She went through a 'finding herself' phase in his early childhood and he was raised by his father and his stepmother who had legal custody. His stepmother, Florence, is an angel and, in many ways, I consider her my mother-in-law. We have always been very close and Devon would go to her for advice.

"Because Devon's mother missed out on so much of his childhood, I think she was trying to be a mother to him after he was married with a vengeance, and really marking her territory. It felt as if she wanted me out, so she could be the only woman in his life. She already had to compete with a beloved stepmother and, in some ways, she was a stepmother herself. His stepmother Florence's advice to Devon was that we had to present a united front. I think this was the best advice we could have ever gotten, and it was such a relief to Devon.

"For Devon, it was like a license to a freedom he had never felt. He had always felt incredibly responsible for his mother. He believed that he had deserted her when he moved in with his dad, even though the move was her idea. His mother has no one but Devon. Her parents are dead, her siblings no longer talk to her, and she is truly alone in the world.

"At one point things seemed to be going smoothly," Mariette remembered. "We came up from Florida to visit his mother in Worcester. We went out to see some friends and when we returned to his mother's house, she had left a note on Devon's pillow that said, she 'felt that I should leave, and he should stay.' My parents were about a two-hour drive from Worcester. It was the middle of the night and I was not going to stay in her house another minute. I told Devon I was leaving. That was the big moment. He said, 'I'm coming with you.' And we left his mother's house together. After this, she began to realize that she could not control Devon's life. He and I were a couple and she could not come between us."

Sometimes, the sheer strength of the bond between the partners is the cement that holds a marriage together. Kelsey knew early on that things weren't going to be easy. But her husband's behavior before they were married helped make, as well as save, their marriage. She said, "One of our biggest blowouts was this one Thanksgiving. You have to understand that my mother-in-law never, ever cooks, not even for Thanksgiving. Every year she has people to her house and we order a bunch of pizzas. But for some reason, one year, before we were married, Draca decided she wanted to cook. The only problem was she didn't have any pots and pans. So, I brought all of my cookware to her house. We (I, really) made a huge dinner and she got drunk. When she's drunk, we just have to wait for a bomb to drop.

"Then, apparently, I made some ghastly mistake. I think I failed to properly relay her rules to a game that we were playing, and she stared at me. It wasn't a quizzical, 'What are you talking about?' look, or even an 'I thought that was between us' glare. It was a death stare. The kind of look a ferocious animal, a lion maybe, gives its prey. The kind of look you get while being circled and stalked, just before you become some lucky den's dinner. I was actually terrified of this sixty-five-year-old woman, wondering what the next step was: the guillotine, maybe?

"I asked, 'Why are you looking at me like that?' She replied, 'I'm not looking at you in any way,' but she said this as if blood was pouring out from between her teeth. I must have looked petrified, because my husband, my then boy-friend, who is utterly conflict-avoidant, got up from his chair to defend me. He demanded to know why she was intimidat-ing me like that. She held to her claim of 'I didn't say any-thing.' He actually shouted at her for the first time in his life. He said, 'You want to know what your stare *sounded* like? It *sounded* LIKE THIIIIIS!' And *he* roared at *her* like a lion! That standoff with his mom impressed me so much, I decided to marry him. Much to her chagrin.

"But," Kelsey remarked, "our wedding brought its own set of delights from Draca. As far as we were concerned, it went off without a hitch. We got married at our farm in Wyoming. We were enthralled, and thought everyone else, especially our family, was too. It wasn't until after we returned from our honeymoon that we started to get the real skinny on what went on during the wedding.

"I'm fairly sure that my mother-in-law, Draca, was the only one stirring up trouble at our wedding, but all by herself she did some significant damage. She hates all social events because of her profound anxieties and social phobias. So, she drinks to let off steam; that sets the stage.

"She went up to my husband's best friend who introduced us when we were kids, and said, in a ferocious voice, 'Hey, thanks for introducing them. Too bad they didn't listen to you when you begged them to break up!'"

I have to admit that, even when I found out about her social outrages, they didn't surprise me. Embarrass me? Yes. Surprise me? No.

"In some ways, being able to talk about her atrocious behavior with my husband helped us to create a stronger bond in our marriage. That which doesn't kill you . . . makes you stronger, right?"

Accepting an Unacceptable Situation

In marriages where the mother-in-law's interference is exceptional and detrimental, there is sometimes a moment when the decision to stay or leave must be made. Some marriages have been lost to bad in-law relationships, and others thrive in spite of in-laws from Hell. In fact, Gloria Horsely, when interviewed in 1997, said that in her research, she found that 70 percent of couples who divorced in their first year of marriage named in-law problems as a major factor in their breakups.

"My relationship with my mother-in-law is a work-in-progress," remarked Portia. "It began on very rocky ground, and I did not expect to have any sort of relationship with her at all, long-term, because of her rejection of me as a woman of color. Matters are now considerably easier, but this new era of 'détente' feels tentative and fragile. There are many things that remain unspoken, and a lot of material remains unprocessed, emotionally speaking.

"Since the ugly early episodes, things have improved immeasurably between us, and she has been a guest at my house several times, but each time the opportunity comes up for me to go to her home, I come up with one excuse or another to prevent the visit.

"In the early days of my marriage, I believed that my mother-in-law didn't really hate me as much as she pretended to; that she was playing a role she felt was expected of her by her community. Oh, she would work herself up into a real hateful frenzy, all right, and she spouted all kinds of spiteful invectives, but a tiny voice inside of me kept whispering, 'This is just for show.' Since she has changed so much, I think now that the little voice was right.

"I have no idea why this sudden transformation occurred, only guesses. Perhaps my father-in-law's ill health caused her to reassess some of her choices. Maybe she was just tired of fighting, especially since her son's marriage to me continued as a strong union. The passage of time? Her visit to the Vatican and the Pope? Who knows?"

Mariette noted, "When our twins were born, my mother-in-law finally saw how she would be the 'odd man out' if she continued behaving the way she had been doing. Also, she got some professional help and started using antidepressant medications. It's amazing how an outsider was able to help her view her relationship with her son.

"She still tries to throw her weight around. It's weird, it's like she wants to have control of our plans, even if they don't include being with her. It's as if she doesn't want anyone else to be in our lives. She'll insist we should spend a holiday with her, reminding us that it is her turn. This happens most often if we've made plans. Last Christmas, for example, we were scheduled to go to Devon's stepmother's house. Florence always has other kids there and the twins love to see their cousins. My mother-in-law insisted that we had to cancel our plans to visit Florence and come to see her. So we did. Two days before Christmas, she informed us that she would be going to her friend's house for Christmas instead. She also mentioned she hadn't gotten around to getting the twins any presents and 'really didn't need the headache.' We had to scramble to put together a holiday for the twins. It was too late, and we were too embarrassed, to go to Florence's. This was a deliberate attempt to spoil our plans. I am sure Florence would have been glad to see us, but at that point we stayed home. Now we just try to navigate carefully through my mother-in-law's twists and turns."

Kelsey agreed with Mariette. "Over the years, I have become very Zen-like about my mother-in-law. I have learned incredible strategies for avoiding conflict with her. I now know when to flatter, when to shut up, when to reveal, when to try to help, and when to just go away. For the most part it works, save for a few annual fights. They usually involve her acting as if she knows my husband best and trying to protect him from me, a point of contention I just cannot seem to rise above. Maybe after thirty years, I'll be able to transcend even that."

Severing Ties

Sometimes, matters go beyond redemption. What may seem navigable becomes a shipwreck. There are also times when severing ties provides a needed break that may not, in fact, be a permanent one. This is not a solution for everyone, but in the daughter-in-law story that follows, such a break gave the couple the needed time and distance from the mother-in-law to regroup and reapproach their situation.

Early in her marriage, Portia found that she didn't want any contact at all with her mother-in-law. "After that one visit to her home before I was married," she noted, "I didn't return for two years after the birth of my first child. There was no contact between us whatsoever, and, apparently, no one was permitted to speak my name in her presence!

"When my first child was born, she told my husband that he was free to come and visit her, but not 'her,' and not 'him' [meaning the baby]. I probably will always resent her for that, no matter how 'good' our relationship ever becomes. That comment struck me like a dagger to the heart. Nikos said that if we, his wife and child, were not invited, then he wouldn't visit her either. His mother said that she didn't need to see him, so long as she knew he was all right. He did keep in contact with her by phone, and that was a bit rough for me, but he and I do things differently. I accepted that, even though it was hard. This was very hard for him. He did not visit her again until we all went together a couple of years later. I let Nikos convince me to give her another chance."

Unlike Portia's strong bond with her husband, Kadijah's bond with her husband was breached. So influential was her mother-in-law in her marriage that Kadijah found the only way to get away from her was total escape. "Oh, my mother-in-law and I had a terrible relationship," she said, "On the surface it looked like we were wonderful friends. But it was a dishonest and mistrustful relationship. Her poison permeated everything, including my marriage.

"She was supercritical with a smile on her face. She encouraged her son to separate from me. She insinuated to him that I was unreliable and untrustworthy. My response was to avoid her. I was very reticent about anything I told her, but I spoke poorly of her to her son. I told him I thought she was mentally ill and that she was trying to kill our relationship. In a funny kind of way she did. She planted the seeds of doubt in his mind, and he used that vision to interpret my behavior. The whole thing blew up in our faces. It was, and still is, very sad."

Ursula went through several stages of severing ties with her mother-in-law. It took her entire marriage of twenty-five years to complete the process. The first phase happened in the middle of winter. "My mother-in-law was taking her daughter down to Chelsea to her piano lesson," she remembered. "I asked for a lift. As we drove, I saw we were about to be hit by another car, and I grabbed my brother-in-law. He and I were thrown from the back seat of the car into the snow, and I was taken to hospital. The insurance man came and said they would pay to have my glasses fixed. He wrote a check for £15, but my mother-in-law said she wanted the check. By way of explanation she said, 'If it hadn't been for you making us wait, the accident would never have happened.' I was shocked! I knew I had to get away from her influence."

Ursula left her marriage only when her youngest kids had reached adolescence. She discovered then the extent of her mother-in-law's animosity. "After twenty-five years," she explained, "I had had enough. I moved out. I got my own apartment. I got a job. My husband told me he would never leave his mother's house, so I left. I tried, unsuccessfully, to explain to the children that I had to go, but that I loved them and would always stay in touch with them. My mother-in-law was livid with rage. Her attitude was 'How dare she leave *my* house!' When I divorced her son, she declared me dead. She wanted to bury me after the divorce. In a way she did, symbolically. She told my kids, 'You don't have a mother anymore. She died.'"

Should You Stay or Should You Go?

Some of the daughters-in-law quoted above had little help in navigating their disturbing relationships. Short of being physically abused or needing police protection, these women were emotionally battered. When they had to interact with their mothers-in-law, they were painful encounters. As in many abusive relationships, some daughters-in-law saw no way out.

Interestingly, we found that all of the women whom we interviewed, who believed that their relationships with their mothers-in-law were ugly at the core, either have divorced or have created an intense, unbreakable bond with their husbands. There was little middle ground. Unlike "bad" mother-in-law/daughter-in-law relationships, the truly unbearable relationships either succeed in contaminating the marital connection, or, through adversity, aid in the creation of an even stronger union.

Where Do You Go from Here?

1. **Damage control.** Don't wait to assess your situation. If your spousal relationship is fragile, you must examine the fault line. Take a step back and evaluate what is happening.

2. **Look at your partner.** If your relationship with your mother-in-law is jeopardizing your marriage, first address the strength of your bond with your spouse.

3. **Do not put yourself in danger.** Be aware. Compromises will be plentiful in the most traumatic of these situations. But do not allow yourself to be victimized.

4. **Don't condemn without a trial.** As you have clearly seen, no relationship is perfect and some are downright bad. But most have room for improvement. Even the worst can be made acceptable if past transgressions can be put safely in the past. Don't misread "awful" for "unbearable."

5. **Remember she is your husband's mother.** This is a profound relationship and he has spent a lifetime safeguarding it. Even if you see maladaptive patterns in the relationship between your spouse and his mother, do not try to destroy it. Be patient and help to foster a better environment with your spouse.

6. **Do get professional help.** Don't hesitate to seek intervention to really comprehend and respond to your specific circumstances.

7. **Know when enough is enough.**

Summary Questions

* *If your mother-in-law were to talk to a confidante of hers about you, how do you think she would characterize your relationship?*

* *Although this question is only for you, and you may never share your thoughts with another, from your own experience what advice would you give to a future daughter-in-law?*

* *Would you still classify your relationship (good, bad, ugly) as you did before you read this book and answered these questions?*

Advice from Daughters-in-Law to Daughters-in-Law

Nel: Realize that your husband's mother is going to play a part in your life and that accepting her and cultivating a good relationship with her will help to maintain the peace in your marriage.

Nina: Think for yourself, try to be reasonable, and look at your mother-in-law for who she is.

Doris: Help your husband separate from his family and establish his home with you. Be respectful of your in-laws, but be an adult and expect to be treated like one. Request of your husband help in understanding his mother.

Sophia: Marry someone who has a healthy, loving relationship with his mother. That way, if he's nice, his mother probably will be too.

Mariette: The best advice I received about dealing with a demanding mother-in-law was for my husband and me to always present a "united front." Of course, it is great to have a sense of humor about the whole thing, after all, she is the mother of my husband and the grandmother of my children *and* I'm stuck with her.

Lahna: Try to be aware of the separation between them and you.

Ellen: Make sure you are the number one person in your husband's life and he knows how to show it. If it is a choice of making you feel loved and honored above his family's demands, no matter how insignificant or great, if it causes you unhappiness, his mother's or father's or siblings' requests should be altered or abandoned.

Lea: Always encourage a good relationship between your spouse and his mother, even when, at times, a situation does not include you.

Jess: Try to develop some shared interests with your mother-in-law, things you both truly enjoy. Then, when and if difficult times come, you still have something to do together or talk about to help you to feel connected and caring.

Nancy: My advice to other daughters-in-law is to be kind and remember that your mother-in-law is your husband's mother, and that she can't be all bad to have had him and to have made him into the man you love.

Tsong: Remember, no matter how difficult your mother-in-law is, you can survive as long as your husband makes it clear that you are the one who matters most.

Estelle: If you find yourself acting weird around your mother-in-law, try to remember that that is what she sees and that is how she thinks you really are. How can she get to know you and understand you if you are putting on a different face in front of her than you do for the rest of the world?

Ursula: Try not to let your mother-in-law's dislike for you color your relationship with your partner. If your mother-in-law did not approve of the relationship or if she has a chip on her shoulder, try to be strong and help your partner to be strong by making your spousal relationship secure and solid.

Larrissa: If your husband's mother waited on him hand and foot when he was a child, be prepared to do the same (or hire someone to help you)!

Fawn: Look carefully at the family of your spouse and his relationship with his mother. If he's always trying to please her then *run run run!*

Joy: Find creative and constructive ways to take the edge off your emotion and then respectfully approach your mother-in-law with complaints or concerns.

Nadja: One thing that helped was that I really did not care much from the beginning what my relationship was going to be. I hoped it would be good, but I did not worry about it.

Sharon: Don't try to turn your husband against his mother. She's his mother . . . and even if you don't like her, they love each other. Try to make the best of it for everyone's sake.

Portia: Remember, you cannot have a good relationship with your partner if your bad relationship with your mother-in-law gets in the way. But you can have a good relationship with your husband despite your bad relationship with your mother-in-law if the two of you, you and your spouse, are bonded together, so tightly connected, that no one, not even his mother, can tear you apart.

Rivkah: Be gentle when talking to your husband about his mother. But do talk.

Juanita: I think understanding your husband's relationship with his mom is important for understanding how your husband will deal with women.

Kadijah: Remember when you marry that you are marrying a family, not only the son.

References

Apter, Terri. 1999. Mothers-in-law and daughters-in-law: Friendship at an impasse. Research paper. Clare Hall, University of Cambridge, England.

————.1991. *Altered Loves: Mothers and Daughters During Adolescence*. New York: Ballantine.

Arnstein, Helene S. 1985. *Between Mothers-in-Law and Daughters-in-Law*. New York: Dodd, Mead & Company.

Barash, Susan Shapiro. 2001. *Mothers-in-Law and Daughters-in-Law: Love, Hate, Rivalry, and Reconciliation*. New Jersey: New Horizon Press.

Broude, Gwen J. 1994. *Marriage, Family and Relationships: A Cross-Cultural Encyclopedia*. Santa Barbara, CA: Santa Barbara Series Encyclopedias of the Human Experience.

Duvall, Evelyn M. 1954. *In-Laws Pro and Con*. New York: Association Press.

Fischer, Lucy Rose. 1983. Mothers and mothers-in-law. *Journal of Marriage and the Family* 45(1):187-192.

Gottman, John M., and Nan Silver. 1999. *The Seven Principles for Making Marriage Work*. New York: Crown Publishers.

Horsely, Gloria. 1997. Interview in *Men's Health*. The other parent trap, by Ron Geraci and Duane Swierczynski. *Men's Health* 12(2):54. March.

Jackson, Jacqueline, and Linda Berg-Cross. 1988. Extending the extended family: The mother-in-law and daughter-in-law relationship of black women. *Family Relations* 37:293-297.

Kassem, Layla. 2001. Personal communication.

Marotz-Baden, Ramona, and Deane Cowan. 1987. Mothers-in-law and daughters-in-law: The effects of proximity on conflict and stress. *Family Relations* 36:385-390.

Psaris, Jett, and Marlena S. Lyons. 2000. *Undefended Love*. Oakland, CA: New Harbinger Publications.

Quick, Barbara. 2000. *Under Her Wing: The Mentors Who Changed Our Lives*. Oakland, CA.: New Harbinger Publications.

Rosten, Leo. 1968. *The Joys of Yiddish*. New York: Pocket Books/Washington Square Press.

Rozakis, Laurie E. 1998. *The Complete Idiot's Guide to Dealing with In-Laws*. New York: Simon and Schuster Macmillan Company, Alpha Books.

Stirling, Paul. 1965. *The Nature of Human Society: Turkish Village*. 1994. Canterbury, England: Centre for Social Anthropology and Computing. University of Kent.

Statistical Abstractions of the United States. 2000. The National Data Book, 120th Edition. Live Births, Deaths, Marriages, and Divorces 1950-1998 (Table 77). Washington, D.C: U.S. Government Printers Office.

Stryker, Sheldon. 1955. Adjustment of family offspring to their parents. *American Sociological Review* 20: 149-153.

Telushkin, Rabbi Joseph. 1991. *Jewish Literacy*. New York: William Morrow & Company.

Yuan, Dong Da Ci Dian. 2000. The Far East Chinese/English Dictionary. Taipei: U.S. International, Inc./Far East Book Company.

Eden Unger Bowditch is a published author, a freelance writer, and the editor of *The Urbanite Magazine*, a Baltimore magazine that addresses urban issues. She lives in Baltimore with her husband and their two children.

Aviva Samet, Psy.D., is a clinical psychologist. She directed the department of family programs at a large Chicago hospital and has special expertise and interest in family dynamics and interpersonal psychotherapy. Aviva is currently in private practice and lives with her husband in Chicago.

Some Other New Harbinger Titles

The Deepest Blue, Item DPSB $13.95

The 50 Best Ways to Simplify Your Life, Item FWSL $11.95

Brave New You, Item BVNY $13.95

Loving Your Teenage Daughter, Item LYTD $14.95

The Hidden Feelings of Motherhood, Item HFM $14.95

The Woman's Book of Sleep, Item WBS $14.95

Pregnancy Stories, Item PS $14.95

The Women's Guide to Total Self-Esteem, Item WGTS $13.95

Thinking Pregnant, Item TKPG $13.95

The Conscious Bride, Item CB $12.95

Juicy Tomatoes, Item JTOM $13.95

Facing 30, Item F30 $12.95

The Money Mystique, Item MYST $13.95

High on Stress, Item HOS $13.95

Perimenopause, 2nd edition, Item PER2 $16.95

The Infertility Survival Guide, Item ISG $16.95

After the Breakup, ATB $13.95

Claiming Your Creative Self, Item CYCS $15.95

The Self-Nourishment Companion, Item SNC $10.95

Serenity to Go, Item STG $12.95

Spiritual Housecleaning, Item SH $12.95

Goodbye Good Girl, Item GGG $12.95

Under Her Wing, Item WING $13.95

Call **toll free, 1-800-748-6273,** or log on to our online bookstore at **www.newharbinger.com** to order. Have your Visa or Mastercard number ready. Or send a check for the titles you want to New Harbinger Publications, Inc., 5674 Shattuck Ave., Oakland, CA 94609. Include $4.50 for the first book and 75¢ for each additional book, to cover shipping and handling. (California residents please include appropriate sales tax.) Allow two to five weeks for delivery.

Prices subject to change without notice.